Astrology and Childhood

PETER WEST

LONDON
HOUSE

First published in Great Britain in 1999 by
LONDON HOUSE
114 New Cavendish Street
London W1M 7FD

A catalogue record for this book is available
from the British Library

ISBN 1 902809 22 X

Edited and designed by DAG Publications Ltd, London.
Printed and bound by Biddles Limited,
Guildford, Surrey.

Contents

Introduction

Astrology has existed for a very long time. Although not widely appreciated, it was the precursor of modern astronomy. Curiously, there is hardly an astronomer alive these days who has a good word for this ancient art-science.

Astrology is neither a science nor an art: it is both. The mechanics of its science have been harmonised with the techniques of the art of interpretation. Together, they produce the most fascinating study into people, or an insight into the events or other matters for which the horoscope was created. Thus, it is an art-science.

Some 6,000 years ago – or perhaps even earlier – the ancient Sumerians began a systematic observation of the heavens and soon realised the stars and their study ('astro' plus 'ology') coincided with the known seasons and other regular and cyclic phenomena. Their beliefs began to be recorded.

At first, these early astrologers came from the largely religious leaders, whose real work was usually concealed in secrecy. In those days, few people could write, let alone read, which is a partial explanation for how the secrecy was maintained for so long. In addition, not everyone would have been allowed access to this secret knowledge because these astrologer/priests also wanted to preserve this special emerging persona. The ordinary people not only believed that these newly emerging leaders understood the messages of the heavens and the gods, but that they communicated with them as well as they sought their divine guidance.

These new astrologers were not fools either. They surely did nothing to offset the beliefs of the common folk and almost certainly spread a few rumours of their own to protect their position in the hierarchy.

Of course, Sumeria was not the only culture or country involved. At about the same time in other countries, astrologer/priests began

Astrology
and Childhood

Alternatives
Life Options for Today

a speedy rise to power in both the eastern and western hemispheres. Despite the many differences of these individual cultures, much of what they believed and began to write about was reasonably consistent, given the situation of the period. They all believed that the Sun, Moon and planets or 'wandering stars' were the homes of the gods. The priests gave them names and thought that by their observations they might just possibly work out the will of the gods in order to counsel those who came for advice, usually the ruler of the country or the very rich.

Astrology has not really looked back since. While it has had a fairly chequered history throughout the years, much of what these ancient astrologers decreed still holds true today, but modified by passing time. They have a very special place in history.

Today, astrologers may be said to be divided into two separate and quite distinct categories, the theoretical and the practical. The former study all manner of ideals and philosophies of this fascinating science with constant research work. This has been greatly helped with the development of the personal computer.

These researchers and their findings, especially in this day and age, have been widely accepted by the latter who, quite frankly, often tend to take many of the new ideas to use in the best and most practical manner they can. In fairness, almost all of them keep statistical records that are of great use to both schools.

It is from this constant exchange of information that the whole study and public interest have been kept alive and flourishing. Astrology is used for an incredibly wide variety of purposes. By far and away the most popular is almost certainly natal (birth) or personal astrology, followed by newspaper and magazine columns. People consult astrologers for many reasons – to learn when they might meet a new love and marry, win money, move house or earn promotion. Astrology is widely used in health matters in both the physical and psychological arenas, with encouraging and positive results.

Astrologers are consulted by those in many different spheres of activity: the farming, rural or gardening worlds, how or when to buy, build, plan a new home, or where to locate a new business for the best effect.

These days, astrology is applied to many aspects of business and commercial issues, and is widely accepted by many companies.

While very few openly admit it, these consultations tend to range from personnel selection to planning new schemes and projects such as take-over battles and sales campaigns. In mundane or political matters the list is endless. As there are countless countries with so many opposing factions enshrined in the politics of these nations, it has become almost a way of life for some astrologers who specialise in just this aspect.

In the last few decades, a new range of astrologer/mathematicians have arrived on the scene and have set out to prove astrology through applying statistical knowledge to the study. Whatever the original motive was behind this philosophy does not really matter here because in just about all cases the results completely vindicated the study and application of astrology. At the same time, they raised many new and interesting questions in the practice. Whatever opinion you currently hold, astrology has stood the test of time much against the odds. In England and other countries the Church opposed and banned it for several centuries in the so-called Dark Ages. But still it flourishes, perhaps more than ever today.

Further, it has also helped us partly to understand our immediate surroundings on earth and also the universe – or at least, what we perceive to be the universe from our rather parochial and very earthly point of view.

1

Basic Astrology

Once each year, the Earth travels round the Sun. The other eight planets – Mercury, Venus, Mars, Jupiter, Saturn, Uranus, Neptune and Pluto – also pass round the Sun in about the same plane as the orbit of the Earth.

Astrology is said to be concerned with the relationships between each of these heavenly bodies and events that occur on Earth. All movements of the Sun, Moon and planets are calculated from a geocentric point of view, that is, from Earth.

This planetary plane is more technically known as the ecliptic, the belt or path of the heavens through which the Sun, Moon and planets travel on their individual and everlasting journeys. A more popular name for this orbital phenomenon is the 'zodiac', or the pathway of the animals. It is divided into twelve separate sections known as the signs. These are commonly called Aries, the Ram; Taurus, the Bull; Gemini, the Twins; Cancer, the Crab; Leo, the Lion; Virgo, the Maiden; Libra, the Scales; Scorpio, the Scorpion; Sagittarius, the Archer; Capricorn, the Goat; Aquarius, the Water Carrier; and Pisces, the Fish.

Each of the signs has a correspondence with a planet or planets. These are said to rule that sign, people and things associated with it. Thus, everything is assigned in some way to a sign and a planet or planets. There are some 'dual' rulerships because of new planets that have been discovered and where many astrologers concluded that some of the older rulerships are out of date and that these new planets have better affinities in their place. All of these changes are on-going and been made from what was discovered and accepted throughout the years, a natural progress in any study.

People born as the Sun transits, or passes, through a sign as it does once a year, are popularly called a Sun-Aries or Sun-Taurus, or much more colloquially as an Arian, a Taurean and so on. The dates and times the Sun enters each of the signs vary very slightly each year because astrologers use astronomical, sidereal or star time which differs from normal or 'civil' clock time.

The exact time for when the Sun enters a sign of the zodiac for any year is given in an ephemeris, a publication that shows all the relevant astronomical and astrological data for any year. These appear in many different versions, for example, as an annual, for ten, fifty or even a hundred years. All are published in advance.

The usually accepted dates for the Sun's entry into the signs and the planets said to 'rule' them are shown in this table:

SUN SIGN	DATE OF ENTRY	PLANETARY RULER
Aries	21 March	Mars
Taurus	20 April	Venus
Gemini	21 May	Mercury
Cancer	22 June	Moon
Leo	23 July	Sun
Virgo	23 August	Mercury
Libra	23 September	Venus
Scorpio	23 October	Pluto
Sagittarius	22 November	Jupiter
Capricorn	22 December	Saturn
Aquarius	20 January	Uranus
Pisces	19 February	Neptune

The Sun is either in one sign or another: it cannot be in two at the same time.

The dividing line between any two signs is called the cusp and has lead to people saying, 'I am a cusp baby.' Anybody born very late in one sign – or very early in the next one – would have to refer to an ephemeris to determine exactly where the Sun, or any other planet for that matter, was on their particular date of birth.

For example, those born on 22 November 1994 would have to do this because the Sun left Scorpio to enter Sagittarius at 13.07 hours on that day. People born before this time would be Scorpios whilst those born later than this are Sagittarians. Both are considered to be 'cusp' babies. Those born at such times are special cases and are dealt with more fully later in the book.

The twelve Sun signs are grouped into one of two basic types, the quadruplicities, or qualities, which are linked with leadership and activity, and the triplicities, or elements, that are mostly concerned with feelings and temperament.

Grouped into four signs, the quadruplicities are associated with activity, and are known as the cardinal, fixed and mutable signs.

The cardinal signs are Aries, Cancer, Libra and Capricorn. People born in these signs display qualities of leadership, are always ready to take the lead, direct and make decisions when the prevailing circumstances call for it. Outgoing individuals.

The fixed signs are Taurus, Leo, Scorpio and Aquarius. As the name suggests, these individuals are rather fixed in their ways, quite determined, persistent and stubborn. Stable personalities.

The mutable signs are Gemini, Virgo, Sagittarius and Pisces. Whatever else they may be, such people are flexible, clever, and have a knack of being able to adapt to what is going on around them. Obliging natures.

There are four triplicities, each representing the four elements of fire, earth, air and water. Each contains three signs. Aries, Leo and Sagittarius are the fire signs. These folk are always active in some way and have good leadership qualities. Lively and impatient personalities.

Taurus, Virgo and Capricorn are the earth signs. As a rule, these people display practicality and common sense when dealing with others or faced with decisions. Literally, down-to-earth characters.

The air signs are Gemini, Libra and Aquarius. Nearly always, such individuals have good communication skills, are socially orientated, clever and intellectually perceptive. Always full of ideas.

Cancer, Scorpio and Pisces are the water signs. People of these signs 'feel' their way through life and appreciate the emotional needs of those around them. Sensitive and receptive natures.

The twelve sun signs are also further divided into masculine, or positive signs, and the feminine, or negative signs. The odd numbered signs – Aries, Gemini, Leo, Libra, Sagittarius and Aquarius – are the positive signs. People who belong to any of these are a trifle more self-expressive on average. All the even numbered signs –

Taurus, Cancer, Virgo, Scorpio, Capricorn and Pisces – are the negative signs. People born in them tend to be slightly self-repressive.

The terms 'positive' and 'negative' are meant in their astrological interpretation and not the universally accepted association one might expect. Reading this, you may begin to recognise some of the behaviour patterns that your son or daughter displays or of some your friends and relatives who probably already do so.

However, for some this may not be the case. Astrology is not as straightforward as all that: you need to know more about how it all works.

The interpretation for each of the twelve signs is based on when the Sun is passing through that sign. It does not allow for considerations such as the influence of the Moon or other planets in that sign at the same time as the Sun. This doesn't include their influence when they are in any of the other signs. Nor does it take into account angular relationships, or aspects, that may be formed between them. These angles are called aspects. Some of them are very special and important to astrology.

There are five major aspects – 0°, 60°, 90°, 120° and 180°. These are known respectively as the conjunction, sextile, square, trine and opposition. A wide number of other minor aspects are also employed as well as aspects to special places in a chart. All have their influence on the character and personality of the individual. As a result, there are very few 'pure' Aries or other Sun-sign types. You may have a child who demonstrates completely different characteristics to those described in this particular section. In the next chapter I will show why as we discuss the personal horoscope.

2

The Individual Horoscope

The horoscope, chart, map, nativity, natus, wheel (call it what you will) is a picture of the heavens for the precise moment you were born or for any other event you wish to question. It is the focal point of nearly all astrological calculations and interpretations.

For the chart to be properly personal, you should have the exact moment of birth – year, month, day and time – preferably to within four minutes. Always give the clock time to allow the astrologer to establish the time zone and also to check if a daylight saving programme was in use. You need to furnish the precise location for him to determine the longitude and latitude of your birthplace, so if you were born in a remote place or small village do include the nearest large town or city.

From this information, the astrologer will calculate your personal horoscope. At the end of the exercise it might look something like the example shown on page 14. It all depends on the system he uses and whether it is hand-drawn or a computer print-out. Please see page 15.

In this case, they are both for the same person, a young woman born on 2 October 1974 in Kingston-upon-Thames, Surrey, England at 7.36 in the evening.

The Sun, Moon and all planets have varying strengths and weaknesses dependent on where they are placed in the chart. In addition, the chart itself has strong focal points in terms of meanings.

However, there are so many different points to take into account it simply is not possible to go into them all here. This is simply to show what an astrologer has to do before he makes his judgement.

The twelve Sun-sign descriptions in the chapters on children are based for when the Sun is in that sign – Sun-sign astrology. A similar exercise can be made for when the Moon is in the sign, Moon-sign astrology.

If, for example, the Sun is in Leo and the Moon is in Pisces, the interpretation for the Sun-Leo character would be tempered by the Moon in Pisces. When the planets and other features with their individual and relative positions are also taken into account, the whole picture can change, often quite considerably.

The Sun, Moon and Planets
To illustrate this, a brief meaning of the varying strengths and weaknesses of the Moon and the planets follows. Please note that the Moon and Venus are often referred to as feminine, but Mars and Jupiter as masculine.

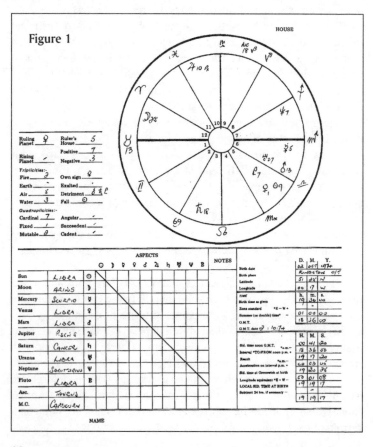

Figure 1

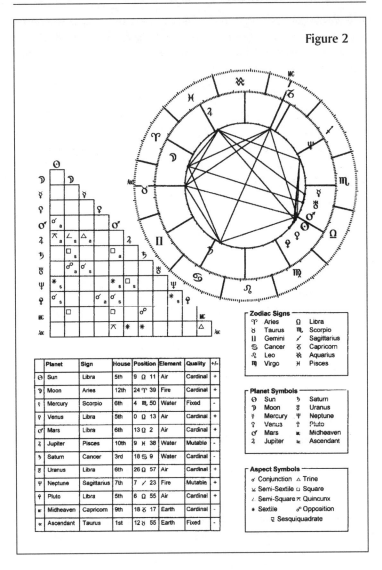

Figure 2

	Planet	Sign	House	Position	Element	Quality	+/-
☉	Sun	Libra	5th	9 ♎ 11	Air	Cardinal	+
☽	Moon	Aries	12th	24 ♈ 39	Fire	Cardinal	+
☿	Mercury	Scorpio	6th	4 ♏ 50	Water	Fixed	-
♀	Venus	Libra	5th	0 ♎ 13	Air	Cardinal	+
♂	Mars	Libra	6th	13 ♎ 2	Air	Cardinal	+
♃	Jupiter	Pisces	10th	9 ♓ 38	Water	Mutable	-
♄	Saturn	Cancer	3rd	18 ♋ 9	Water	Cardinal	-
♅	Uranus	Libra	6th	26 ♎ 57	Air	Cardinal	+
♆	Neptune	Sagittarius	7th	7 ♐ 23	Fire	Mutable	+
♇	Pluto	Libra	5th	6 ♎ 55	Air	Cardinal	+
Ɱ	Midheaven	Capricorn	9th	18 ♑ 17	Earth	Cardinal	-
Ɱ	Ascendant	Taurus	1st	12 ♉ 55	Earth	Fixed	-

Zodiac Signs

♈	Aries	♎	Libra
♉	Taurus	♏	Scorpio
♊	Gemini	♐	Sagittarius
♋	Cancer	♑	Capricorn
♌	Leo	♒	Aquarius
♍	Virgo	♓	Pisces

Planet Symbols

☉	Sun	♄	Saturn
☽	Moon	♅	Uranus
☿	Mercury	♆	Neptune
♀	Venus	♇	Pluto
♂	Mars	Ɱ	Midheaven
♃	Jupiter	Ɱ	Ascendant

Aspect Symbols

☌ Conjunction △ Trine
⊻ Semi-Sextile □ Square
∠ Semi-Square ⚻ Quincunx
∗ Sextile ☍ Opposition
⚼ Sesquiquadrate

The Moon

In essence, the Moon has no real power of her own. She influences our emotional response of the moment, our instinctive reactions to

15

whatever situation we find ourselves in, based on where she is and in relationship, or aspect with, any other planet or planets and parts of the birth chart. She may be considered rather like a chameleon as she reflects these influences.

Mercury

The first planet from the Sun influences communication of kinds. How we think and reason, calculate, then decide on a subsequent course of action depends on where Mercury is placed in the chart and in relationship, or aspect with, any other planet or planets and parts of the birth chart.

Venus

The second planet from the Sun reveals how we relate emotion-ally, socially and artistically. She conditions our tastes, appearance and the styles we come to favour. Venus also indicates how we might negatively react when others or circumstances let us down. It, too, depends on where she is in a chart and in relationship, or aspect with, any other planet or planets and parts of the birth chart.

Mars

This planet influences our physical energy levels, both negatively and positively. Self-assertion, initiative, resistance and how we direct those impulses are also shown by Mars, depending on where it is in a chart and in relationship, or aspect with, any other planet or planets and parts of the birth chart.

Jupiter

We look to this planet to ascertain our moral and ethical nature, sense of purpose, and how we seek to improve ourselves as we progress. Compassion and generosity levels are also shown by Jupiter depending on where it is in a chart and in relationship, or aspect with, any other planet or planets and parts of a birth chart.

Saturn

Influences our levels of personal responsibility and discipline, how we acquire them and live within the restriction imposed by our sense of limitation. It also shows how we may best find order and security, depending on where it is in the chart and in relationship, or aspect with, any other planet or planets and parts of the birth chart.

Uranus

Shows our creative senses and how we may best express ourselves. It reveals an inner, natural rebel streak where we may not follow convention. It illustrates how or when we might break free to seek out others like us, depending on where it is in a chart and in relationship, or aspect with, any other planet or planets and parts of the birth chart.

Neptune

Influences the way we choose to experience our needs, wants, dreams and fantasies. It can also demonstrate how we tend to deceive not only ourselves but others in the pursuit of these ideals. Our ego and emotional stability are also shown depending on where it is in a chart and in relationship, or aspect with, any other planet or planets and parts of the birth chart.

Pluto

This planet will show how you exhibit your innermost convictions and compulsions. Obsessions and your desire for control or power are also indicated. Change, or a way to transform your life, will always be indicated by Pluto, depending on where it is in a chart and in relationship, or aspect with, any other planet or planets and parts of the birth chart.

The Houses

Modern astrologers have a choice of many types of house division systems. Most generally tend to use Equal House. All of these explanations are based upon this.

As a rule, most birth charts are divided into twelve segments or houses. Each house has its own special meaning and may be taken roughly equivalent to the signs of the zodiac. But when planets are sited in the houses, a dual correspondence between the houses, signs and planets occurs.

For example, the Moon rules Cancer and is said to be powerfully placed if it should fall in the fourth house because this corresponds with Cancer in the natural order of the zodiac. This means that the fourth house is the natural house of Cancer. In the same way, Aries corresponds with the first house, Taurus with the second house, and so on to Pisces, the natural twelfth house.

As the Earth travels on its daily path round the Sun, the signs move through the houses at varying speed. Thus, at any time one of these signs will be on the first house cusp. This special part of the chart, and in particular the degree of the sign, is called the Ascendant. Astrologers everywhere hold this special point in very high regard.

The Ascendant, the whole of the house and each subsequent house, has an affinity with certain special areas of a person's life. The planets and signs fall within a house's sphere of activity according to their position in the horoscope. Mostly, the meanings of the houses are largely traditional, but tempered by the experience of the astrologer and modern research.

Each of the first six houses are said to relate by polarity with the second six. The first is linked with the seventh, the second with the eighth, etc. Briefly, here are the meanings associated with each house.

The First House

Our basic personality, how we prefer the world to see us, and how we actually do so. Our disposition, temperament and, to an extent, our physical appearance.

It is said that the sign, its ruling planet or any planet in this house wields an extremely strong influence on our physical well-being and general behavioural patterns throughout life. For most astrologers, it is the most important part of the horoscope.

The Second House

This relates to all income and expenditure, material possessions and overall responses to our financial needs and wants. Some say this house can also have a bearing on our feelings and emotions when we decide on the best way to serve our own interests as well as those of others in such matters.

The Third House

The sign on the cusp and any planets in the house indicate how we relate to our brothers and sisters, our immediate environment and usual daily contacts. It also shows how we influence these people and how they may affect us. Further, it rules short journeys and all forms of communication.

The Fourth House

This is mostly concerned with our domestic environment, people in it, both past, present and, indeed, in the future. It also rules our attitude to buying or selling domestic property, connections with our roots and ancestors, local and national pride. Planets in this house influence our innermost personal and private thinking.

The Fifth House

Planets in this house shape our creativity and self-expression, the way we enjoy the pleasures and amusements of life in matters of sex, pregnancy and our attitudes towards children as a result. New ventures, how we spend our leisure time, relationships with the people involved, animals, pets and speculation.

The Sixth House

This house, and any planets in it, rules the way we accept our responsibilities in employment, service to others and how we may adjust to the everyday realities of life. It is very much concerned with personal health and hygiene, and related matters like diet and fitness. Our personal appearance is influenced from here.

The Seventh House

Shows how we respond to all forms of relationships and partnerships, whether personal or business orientated. It is often referred to as the house of marriage and can show a future spouse in some circumstances. Legal problems and litigation are ruled by the seventh house. Planets here may show why or with whom.

The Eighth House

Traditionally, this house has always been associated with the end of life, wills, legacies, joint – or other people's – possessions or money.

Big businesses such as banks, insurance houses or even the Stock Exchange and how the individual is affected by them may be shown here. Sexual attitudes will also be indicated.

The Ninth House
Here, the attitude of the individual to the realms of education, religious meaning and philosophy is shown. People and places abroad as well as long-distance travel are also referred to from this house. Strongly placed planets here could show that the subject might take up law as a career.

The Tenth House
The cusp of the tenth house is called the mid-heaven and is almost as important as the ascendant. Here we see how we relate to all external and material aspects of life. Ambition, career, reputation and personal status, always matters of importance no matter what we say, are to be delineated from here.

The Eleventh House
This is the house of associations, groups and societies, and shows the importance, or otherwise, that we place on our non-personal social life. We see how we, as individuals, tend to get along with those with whom we must or wish to associate with by virtue of our social position or occupation.

The Twelfth House
Strictly speaking, this house, together with any planets therein, shows the general state of our psychological well-being like inner fears, dreams and secret fantasies. Our attitudes to places of seclusion such as asylums, hospitals or prisons. Anything that inhibits self-expression or our depth of understanding of life.

All the variations of these individual house meanings, planetary placements and signs on the house cusps have a bearing on the way our character and personality is formed. In addition, there are many other features that an astrologer has to take into account when he comes to judge the nativity, far too many to list here, but all important in their own way.

With these brief explanations in mind, perhaps you can now see why some children fail to respond the way we expect when we learn of their Sun sign. Other factors are obviously influencing them and their development. The next step to help you try to understand your child better is to have his birth chart created, but if this is not possible, why not visit your local library and look in an ephemeris for his birth date particulars? Note the position of the Sun, Moon and the planets and apply all the foregoing interpretations because with these basic hints and tips you will be much better prepared than most for your child's actions as and when they occur.

The Aspects

While the Sun, Moon and planets make their journeys through the heavens, at any moment in time they are likely to form an angle or series of angles to each other. When the picture of the heavens for any moment is recorded in the birth chart, an angle or series of angles may be formed to major points in that map. These angles are commonly called aspects, and there are a great many of them. In essence, some are natural, others man-made.

In a purely astronomical sense all aspects are created by certain angular distances from one planet to another as viewed from the Earth – geocentric aspects. For an astrologer to be able to understand and interpret them is very important because it qualifies and quantifies their relative strengths and weaknesses in these relationships to one another in addition to their basic house and sign position in a chart.

As explained, there are five major aspects. Traditionally, these have always been divided into good or bad, hard or soft, or easy or difficult types. For example, the 180° opposition angle, created when the 360° picture of the heavens is divided by two, has always been regarded as stressful, creating tension, making life a little difficult. When you think of two or even more bodies opposing one another the very word suggests some kind of conflict must be involved.

The conjunction, when two or more planets are placed together in a chart, suggests their energy will become focalised because of their proximity. The same principles are applied to all of the other aspects.

To make an astrologer's life even more difficult, much depends on whether these aspects are approaching, exact or departing. An approaching aspect is when planets become sufficiently close to one another to begin to create an aspect. This becomes exact when they are precisely together. Departing aspects are so-called as they begin to pull away from each other's influences.

The allowable distance for an approaching or departing aspect is called an orb. Therefore, the closer the orb, the more influence exerted by the planets involved. The wider apart they are, the less effect they have on each other.

Opinions have always differed as to the degree of orb allowable. It is left entirely to the individual astrologer. In addition to these major, or more influential aspects, there is also a wide number of minor aspects that are open to use by some astrologers or ignored by others. Again, it is according to personal taste.

All of these aspects have their influence on the character and personality of the subject or matter under review. This is one of the many reasons why there are very few so-called pure Aries or other Sun-sign types. This continuous interplay of the planets with each other is liable to distort the purity of any Sun-sign personality.

Finally, having explained all the different aspects, places and positions the planets might occupy and whereby they may or not be influenced, the astrologer has also to note whether the planet does not make or receive aspects. This also causes its influence to be stronger or weaker depending on the position in the chart.

All of this accounts for why you might easily have a child who demonstrates completely different characteristics to those I have described in that particular Sun-sign section. The house and sign position of a planet, together with the many possible aspects pushing and pulling here, there and everywhere, really does ring the changes when it comes to interpreting the birth chart.

3
The Aries Child

Dates	Circa	21 March – 20 April
Ruler		Mars
Symbol		The Ram
Metal		Iron
Colour		Bright Red
Part of the Body		Head and Face
Natural House		First
Classification		Cardinal – Fire – Positive

 An Aries baby makes his presence felt from the moment he is born: you know he has arrived by the raucous noises coming from his cot – a sound you are not likely to forget in a hurry!

Aries is a Cardinal Fire sign and that means action. These little ones are rarely still for very long, perhaps just enough to catch their breath before they plunge headlong into their next adventure. They are energetic, boisterous, individualistic little characters who always seem to be accident-prone and determined to give their parents a heart attack at least twice a day.

These youngsters require very firm discipline from the word go! If you learn to channel their energies early and constructively and guide their feet on to the paths of learning, they will repay your (exhausted) patience a thousandfold. But allow your young Ram to have his head, you and your partner will almost certainly end up asking each other why you had him in the first place.

An Aries child must never be allowed to get bored for he can be domineering, headstrong, tactless and exasperating beyond belief at times. These negative traits are extremely difficult to contend with, but with suitable encouragement his positive points will predominate and you find yourself with an enterprising, enthusiastic, independent and fiercely loyal child who exhibits good leadership qualities even at an early age.

Aries children need an environment where they may safely explore. Constructive, colourful and noisy toys help to stimulate their fertile minds. However, they must also have plenty of rest – perhaps more than children of other signs – but will only take it when they want.

Their tastes are fairly wide-ranging when it comes to food. They are inclined to eat almost anything put in front of them, provided it is not mushy. They prefer to eat only when they are hungry and certainly when they want to. Unfortunately, this may not necessarily be at meal times. Aries children do not take very kindly to having anything imposed upon them, especially regular habits.

In the early days, much care and patience are necessary to bring them round to your way of thinking and to persuade them to conform to your wishes.

Health-wise, Aries youngsters are susceptible to fevers and very sensitive to changes of temperature. Make sure you wrap your little Ram up warmly before you venture out of doors. The head, ears, eyes and teeth are their weakest points, often having frequent, but not serious, minor accidents. They always seem to be covered in bumps, bruises and cuts, mostly caused by carelessness, so watch out for their rough-and-tumble games.

As a rule, Aries boys have less sense of responsibility than Aries girls, but both learn very quickly to look after themselves, which serves to make them very independent in later life. However, while still only a few months old, baby Aries will let you know at all times when your parental services are required. His eyes will follow you or any other visual stimulus almost from the moment he is born. Similarly, his awareness of sound is acute very early in life. Highly coloured mobiles that tinkle or chime as they move will be a source of great delight to him.

The little Ram loves any attention from his parents, or anyone else in the family whom he recognises. Baby Aries also enjoys being cuddled, but does not like to feel restricted. Don't hold him too tightly, but do so very, very carefully.

One of the first aspects you notice about your Aries baby is his voice. He learns from the outset how to make his presence felt. Once he realises how easy it is to wield this most powerful weapon, he will demand attention all day, every day.

That tiny little bundle of joy you first brought home has a knack of taking over everything and everybody in his life in a rather short space of time. If you begin to feel the strain and get short-tempered, his toothless little grin will melt your heart and you soon learn to put up with it.

Babies – and young Aries is no exception – are supposed to sleep for about two-thirds of each day, but unfortunately for you, they don't (or won't) do it in one gloriously long session. Instead, they usually take little naps that just do not give you a chance to get anything done around the house in the way you always used to. Most Aries babies (although, unfortunately, not all) sleep for about 14 hours out of 24, but many can develop a taste for all-night slumber before six months are out. They usually also enjoy the odd day-time nap here and there.

Baby Ram begins to move around slightly earlier than most other signs. By four months, he should be able to sit up with the minimum of assistance from an adult. He will now gurgle quite happily with that special greeting he reserves for his mother as he will have started to recognise her as someone very special. He also laughs and smiles a lot.

By six months, he ought to manipulate toys and other small items he favours quite well. Of course, as he now has a quite well-developed sense of taste and smell, much of what he does pick up may find its way to his mouth. Aries children move very swiftly indeed, so be prepared. You are going to have to be very firm from the beginning. He needs to be taught who is the real boss and must learn to respect your authority. However, as is so often the case with an Aries child, this is easier said than done.

At eight months, he should be able to stand up, probably with a little help. By ten months, or earlier in some special cases, he will have achieved some degree of independent movement. Now a new nightmare begins! Baby Aries is an adventurer and remains so all his life. He is endlessly curious and so inquisitive and eager to explore that once he finds he has mastered the art of getting around, he will be off like a shot at every opportunity.

This means that supervision is very important. He needs to know that some things may be touched while others must not, and should be taught to respond immediately to the word 'No!' If he manages to move beyond his normal nursery environment, do ensure that he cannot get into trouble with items adults normally take for granted but which are unfamiliar and dangerous to him, such as electrical appliances, water, or even sharp corners of furniture. Such restrictions on his new-found freedom will not meet with his approval.

In addition, he will be often frustrated with his inability to do things as swiftly or as deftly as he might prefer. Temper tantrums are often the result – and one from a baby Aries really is a sight to behold. But it does not normally last very long, and he will soon be off again on his chosen path in search of new discoveries.

By about 15 months, he will have developed a small vocabulary. He then soon learns to ask questions about everything that catches his ever-alert eye. He has a need to learn, to find out why. Baby Aries likes to live life – he wants to feel he has been there, done that, enjoyed the experience (or not, as the case may be) and certainly got the T-shirt.

Once he has overcome whatever physical obstacles may have been in his way and succeeded in experiencing whatever it was that attracted him, he will remain as active as ever. Make no mistake: this youngster really is always on the move. A child-proof safety gate placed at the top of the stairs is an absolute must. You will probably also want one to keep him from any area such as the fireplace where he may hurt himself or precious items he might damage, like your computer or CD system.

By about two years old, your little Ram will be all over the place. For Aries children, the head and shoulders are among the most vulnerable parts of their little bodies, so please make sure he is never able to pull anything down on top of himself. A guard-rail will be needed along the top of the cooker: electric kettles and any other potentially dangerous household equipment must be kept out of his reach at all times. Try not to leave the iron lying around to cool; don't place ironing draped over a clothes-horse. Protect electric points and ensure none of the heaters in your home can be overturned.

As your child grows older, he has to learn to socialise. This is not always an easy task for the young Ram. He must understand it is important to share, to give and take, and let other children play with his toys and possessions. Brothers and sisters of young Rams will find the ground rules for sharing and playing together are laid down very early on indeed and that learning to rub along together will not be simple for either party! The delicate art of getting on with other people and compromising is something that all children are taught or discover for themselves in the family environment.

Early domestic circumstances surrounding a child always have a bearing on the way he learns to adapt. Do remember that the resultant attitudes and patterns of behaviour starting to develop now will eventually be carried forward into his adult life, although moderated slightly here and there by experience as he matures.

In many cases, adjusting to those around him also means having to learn to negotiate as well . . . and a young Ram is far from happy when put in this position. If forced to negotiate, he usually does so from a very selfish stand-point. Many factors affect his behaviour towards those around him. Perhaps the most important is his position in the family pecking order.

Single Aries children have an in-built level of self-confidence which is also demonstrated by young Rams who are the eldest in the family with several younger siblings. They seem to maintain this self-assurance in almost any circumstances. It will therefore make little difference if your child is strictly disciplined or pampered and spoiled.

Generally speaking, any child who comes second in the family order tends to have a little less confidence and displays slightly more aggression. Usually, this shows when the youngster has to outshine an older brother or sister or needs to prove himself, but this is no problem for a young Ram. If left to make his own way, the Aries child quickly finds his own niche in life and settles, although Aries boys tend to be somewhat lazier than girls as they develop.

As a third child, Aries youngsters learn the hard way, but very quickly indeed. There is often great rivalry between brothers and sisters, and the more there are, the more this will be so. The number three child has to work hard to make his mark on the world even at a very early age, but once again this presents few problems for the young Aries, who usually proves to be quite resourceful and adaptable.

At school, Aries pupils take very quickly to their new-found independence and learn quickly from their mistakes. They readily adapt, add to and discard from their growing stock of experience. Like all children, as they progress they also develop their own behaviour patterns. The speed with which this happens depends on whether the child is basically an introvert or an extrovert.

Let there be no doubt in your mind about this one: almost without exception, Aries children – at whatever age – must be considered extroverts. They are probably the most outgoing and positive personalities of all the signs of the zodiac.

4
The Taurus Child

Dates	Circa	20 April – 21 May
Ruler		Venus
Symbol		The Bull
Metal		Copper
Colour		Green
Part of the Body		Neck and Throat
Natural House		Second
Classification		Fixed – Earth – Negative

As a rule, baby Taureans come into the world in a relatively peaceful manner. Once a routine has been established, they remain quite contented.

Taurus is a Fixed Earth sign. This implies stability, so these children soon become confident and determined. Parents should try not to rush their young Bull, but be patient and allow him to progress at his own pace towards his well-defined goals. As a rule, most Taurus youngsters rarely hurry anywhere.

In the main, these youngsters are strong, robust and healthy, rarely giving cause for concern to their parents except when their legendary stubbornness comes into play. Then there are problems! Discipline is best applied by appealing to the Taurean child's emotions, for pressure and threats rarely work well – if at all. When a young Taurean decides to dig in his heels, playing the heavy-handed parent will never work. And while young Bulls rarely lose their temper, it will do you no good at all if you show yours.

The average Taurean child may appear rather slow to learn, yet his mind absorbs all the information that comes his way. Ideally, you should provide him with a peaceful environment where he can play with educational rather than physically demanding toys. Let him paint, doodle or draw, or just sit there and watch as you go about your daily chores. But make sure you explain what you are doing and why, because that will also interest this intelligent, usually obedient, constructive and basically honest child.

Do not allow young Taurus to become discontented due to a lack of attention on your part or because of poor or uncomfortable surroundings or you will soon find yourself having to deal with a selfish, lazy, indulgent, possessive and obstinate little fiend.

Very young Bulls prefer to have regular habits for they dislike change and need their rest and relaxation periods. They quickly learn when their afternoon nap is due and will let you know if you have forgotten. Often, they simply curl up and go to sleep wherever they are at the time.

These youngsters have a healthy appetite and tend to eat almost anything that is not exotic or unfamiliar. However, never try to feed a baby Bull a dish he may not want or seem not to like. He will reject it out of hand and, just as stubbornly, refuse to eat it.

In health matters, young Taurus is susceptible to inflammations, infections of the throat and weight problems. Also beware of an inclination to put anything and everything into his mouth for he is a very tactile little individual who likes to try everything at least once.

As a rule, young Taurus girls are blessed with more than a fair share of common sense and well able to take care of themselves a lot earlier than their brothers. However, on the whole, the boys are quite sensible and mature early. Almost from the moment he arrives, baby Bulls are attracted by any visual stimulus so you will soon notice that his eyes begin to follow you around.

He is appreciative of touch, and throughout life has highly developed sensory tastes. He loves attention, to touch or be touched by any member of his family and very close friends. He also loves little cuddles, which give him a great sense of security. The young Taurean adores the feeling of arms around him, so hold him firmly. In fact, baby Bulls enjoy all kinds of comfort and security, so make sure his immediate surroundings are warm and settled.

The young Bull dislikes change and anything that is not familiar. He can be possessive, remaining so all his life if he can get away with it. But in the first months, he will make his needs known using the only weapon available – his voice. Once he understands how eagerly you respond, he will assume command despite his age and size, demanding attention all day and every day.

All Taurus babies have an in-built knack of taking control of everything and everybody within a very short space of time. Just as you begin to think you might have laid down a regime to suit you, he will show you what he wants . . . and when he wants it!

In most cases – although, regrettably, not all – baby Bulls soon establish a sleep routine of about 14 hours a day. They also enjoy a few snoozes now and then throughout the day and, with a bit of luck, may begin to sleep through the night any time after about four months.

Baby Bulls tend not to move around too early, having a lazy streak which they indulge as often as possible, and begin to explore slightly later than children of other signs. At about five months, your Taurean child ought to be able to sit up when supported and will start to gurgle or babble happily to his mother. By now he recognises her as someone who looks after his interests almost as much as he would like. He will also laugh and smile a lot.

By six months, he will play with toys or other objects. These should be highly coloured and small so he can hold them comfortably in his hands. If they are noisy as well, so much the better. Taurus offspring enjoy music from an early age as it helps soothe them. Their parents rapidly discover they can use it to help to get them off to sleep at night.

With their highly developed sense of touch and smell, baby Bulls quickly learn to test everything with their mouths, so everything must be spotlessly clean at all times. This is not always easy. Because Taurus is an Earth sign, there is nothing these children like better than playing in the dirt. Fortunately, despite being Earth babies, they also love bath time and playing with water. Once in it, they are comfortable and relaxed, but be prepared for the din when you try to take them out!

Although very young Taurus children tend not to move around a great deal at the beginning, as they develop and grow, you are going to have to be very firm right from the outset. Your baby must learn who the real boss is and be made to respect your authority early – and the earlier the better. This is not easy with a Taurus child: he can be one very stubborn baby. Once used to a routine, you will probably have to move heaven and earth if you want him to change it.

By about nine months, he should be able to stand up, with a little help perhaps. About this time, he will finally start to move around. Now you have a whole new ballgame to play, and supervision will be of paramount importance. Like other children, he must be taught early that some things may be touched while others cannot. You may wish to try reinforcing your message with the gentlest of smacks on the back of his hand, but remember that he is touch-conscious . . . and smacking can work both ways!

Even though he has at last learned to move around, little Taurus tends to stay put and may be quite happy to sit for hours in one place and play with his toys. He is a patient little soul and will sit in his high chair for long periods at a time, watching you go about your chores and listening as you explain what you are doing.

However, he is not overly adventurous or much inclined to explore. Despite this, he has a streak of curiosity and will happily spend time playing with simple puzzles until he succeeds in solving them.

He is also likely to put weight on rather quickly, but this is nothing to worry about, and all perfectly normal for little Bulls.

Once he begins to talk, he will use his small vocabulary to ask what may seem like an interminable series of questions. He much prefers to learn at his own pace and tends to be rather precise and rather selective in his interests. Eventually, he will start to explore. Although doing so fairly slowly at first, you will find a child-proof safety gate at the top of the stairs, or placed across the kitchen doorway, will now really be needed.

By the time he is about two years old, your little Bull is fairly well settled in his ways. He will have found all the comfortable corners in the house, those little niches where he busies himself with whatever interests him at the time.

A young Taurean is not particularly accident-prone, but because of his tactile nature tends to put things in his mouth and could make himself choke. He may overeat and so might suffer from frequent tummy troubles; he is also prone to dental and dietary problems. His other weak features are the ears, nose and throat: keep him well protected from any inflammatory conditions. While under the weather, he will so dislike being uncomfortable and unwell he could actually prolong the problem. He appreciates being cuddled and pampered if sick, but is not the easiest of patients at the best of times.

Learning to socialise is a relatively easy matter for your young Bull. He is fairly easy to get along with, although a hint of selfishness – always common in young children – may show at times. However, he has a caring attitude towards his brothers or sisters, but expects loyalty and honesty in return from members of his family.

The single Taurus child has a good level of confidence, much as he does if he is the oldest when little brothers or sisters come along. Generally speaking, as a second child in the family, the Taurus youngster does not feel the need to outshine his older brother or sister in order to prove himself and so will not suffer from the lack of confidence or increased aggression, which often typify second children. Left to his own devices, he will soon find his niche in life and settle. As they develop, Taurus lads generally seem somewhat lazier than their sisters.

As a third child, a Taurus youngster adapts to his position in life with some difficulty. He likes to socialise, but it may come as a rude surprise to learn what some people are really like as he discovers the hard way that human nature can often show a none-too-pleasant face. He might often realise too late that he has been used.

All 'number three' children have to work hard to make their mark on the world. Although young Taurus is fairly set in his ways, even at a very early age he can be resourceful in attempts to learn to adapt and become compatible with his peers. Of course, once at school the sheer weight of numbers of other children will go a long way to help him develop his level of independence or dependence on others. He may well regard teachers in the light of comparison with either of his parents, with his favourites soon being established.

Taurus children do not always learn from their mistakes as others might. It takes time for them to adapt but as they mature, they discover how to add to and discard from their growing fund of experiences of life. In their dealings with other people, most young Bulls learn to compromise, but are not unknown to add 'strings' to their deals. They develop personal behaviour patterns as all other children, but are less flexible.

Much depends on whether the child is basically an introvert or an extrovert, but there is little doubt that from a very young age the Taurus child is basically introverted. He is rather placid and a little shy. On the plus side, his attitudes to life are usually far from totally negative.

5
The Gemini Child

Dates	Circa 21 May – 21 June
Ruler	Mercury
Symbol	The Twins
Metal	Quicksilver
Colour	Yellow
Part of the Body	Arms, Chest and Lungs
Natural House	Third
Classification	Mutable – Air – Negative

 Gemini is a Mutable Air sign, which suggests mental activity. Gemini babies are usually alert from the moment of birth: they sleep lightly, are very easily distracted and become bored just as easily.

Active all the time, their hands and minds are rarely still. Happiest when they can probe here and investigate there, baby Geminians are as bright as buttons all their waking hours, but need constant stimulation or become fractious.

The art of disciplining the young Gemini needs the patience of a saint and the wisdom of Solomon for these are very intelligent children and, believe it or not, can fool you most of the time. You should attempt to appeal to your child's emotions, but if that fails, try to reason with him. Smacking is unlikely to get you very far. The physical pain may be hardly noticed but merely tolerated until he can get on with whatever it was he was doing before you interfered and spoiled it all. However, the application of love and logic should work wonders, preferably in that order.

The negative traits of any young Gemini are restlessness, deceit, superficiality and erratic behaviour. However, usually their positive characteristics are vivacity and adaptability. They have a vivid imaginative sense, are easy-going and very quick-witted.

If you want to encourage your young Gemini's better nature, ensure that he has bright and interesting surroundings. Provide toys which stimulate and occupy his mind, and books, musical instruments, puzzles or games to challenge his intellect. These help to keep him out of mischief, for a while at least.

Remember that Geminians thrive on all kinds of endless variety. It is what is really needed. Even his diet should be as varied as possible. The same meal offered twice in two days will almost certainly be rejected. Boring! Despite this, a Gemini child has quite a healthy appetite, even though he may not appear to eat a lot, judging from the mess on the floor! His problem is that he simply finds it difficult to sit in one place long enough to get through meal-times. He wants to be off doing something else – and the sooner the better.

There is an old astrological saying that 'You can't keep a good Geminian down.' Repeat this to yourself until engraved firmly on your mind for it will save you lots of problems in later years.

In health matters, these children need adequate rest because they use up their nervous energy very quickly. However, they may not actually go to sleep until quite late no matter how physically tired they are because their minds are still active. This child needs a good, nourishing diet or is liable to all kinds of minor ailments such as colds and chills, and will easily fall prey to all the minor bugs doing the rounds. He is also prone to accidents to his hands, arms and shoulders, not to mention grazed knees on an almost daily basis.

Usually, Geminian boys lack any real sense of responsibility and tend to put off making decisions until the last moment. However, the girls generally have a much more positive attitude.

When your Gemini baby is very small, you have to learn to distinguish his cries for attention and what they mean. Most of the time it will be for the usual requirements, but it may simply be that young Gemini has become bored.

You will discover that his eyes start to follow you around the room almost from the start, but he is equally aware of sound. Many small mobiles, little bells and anything else that makes a sound delight him, provided you make a few changes from time to time. Baby Gemini loves and responds well to any change because of the challenge it brings.

He is insatiably curious, so his early toys should reflect this. Within a few weeks, anything that he can push, pull and move will be welcome. He enjoys all the attention he can get from either of his parents, other family members or close friends. He is keen on little cuddles, but just being near someone else is often enough because he hates being restricted. But when holding him, watch out: this one is a wriggler!

Baby Gemini likes to be on the move. Once mobile, he will be away like a rocket. A large play-pen is ideal, but it may need some extra judicial padding for he tends to bruise easily and incurs lots of little bumps and bruises in his adventures.

Babies are supposed to sleep for about 14 or 15 hours each day, but unfortunately for you, not always in one go. Your little Gemini will indulge in frequent short snoozes, but these are not often quite long enough for you to get chores done in the way you might like.

Baby Gemini begins to sit up with assistance at about four or five months or so. He will also enjoy regular excursions outdoors in his pram. As he does not take very kindly to confinement, he will particularly look forward to this. By six months, he should be able to hold and use toys and other playthings with ease. Like other children, much of what he picks up often finds its way to his mouth. Thus, you must pay very close attention to cleanliness, especially at this early stage.

At eight months, he ought to be able to stand up, initially with a little help, of course. But at about nine months or so, possibly a little earlier in special cases, he will manage to move around – and now a new nightmare starts for you!

Young Geminis can move swiftly, but they often choose to stay put and quite still in a corner for long periods at a time. Somehow, this latter behaviour is the more difficult to deal with. After all, wriggling all over the place is expected, but when he settles in a corner somewhere and does not respond to calls, you may find yourself wrong-footed and at a loss as to what to do. Take comfort: he is not being awkward, but probably totally absorbed in what he is doing to the exclusion of everything else around him. However, be firm. As he becomes older, you will be able to appeal to his sense of fair play. Ask him how he would feel in your shoes. That should do the trick.

Baby Gemini is a naturally inquisitive child. Once able to co-ordinate his movements, he will start to explore. As he is endlessly curious, this can mean anything and anywhere, often restricted only by his inability to do things he has seen others do. This will frequently lead to deep frustration and temper. Temper tantrums may also often be precipitated by the typical Geminian rebel streak, but as a rule they do not normally last long unless restrictions have been placed on him. He will soon come out of it and be off again, discovering pastures new.

Once he begins to talk, which may be earlier than most, a Gemini toddler should develop a fair vocabulary quite early. By about eighteen months, he will be asking all sort of questions. While you may be able to fob off other little ones with a brief or trite answer, you certainly won't get away with it with this little chap. He wants answers and explanations as well. He needs to learn, to find out why: it is all part of the Geminian experience. They simply will not give up until they get what they want, and that can take up a lot of their effort, energy and time.

Because this child is always on the move, one really must install child-proof safety gates worthy of the Gemini and his capacity for exploration at the top of the stairs, or around any hazardous area. You will also need a guard-rail along the top of the kitchen stove. Electric kettles and other potentially dangerous household equipment must always be kept out of his reach. Protect electric points, and ensure portable heaters cannot be overturned.

By the time he is about two years old, this youngster will have been all over the place, so quite a few vulnerable areas on his little body probably bear the scars to show it. Make sure that his arms, hands and shoulders all have extra protection for while little Geminis are no more accident-prone than children of the other signs, they certainly have their moments.

An Air sign, they are very sensitive to colds and chills, and react adversely to sudden temperature changes. If you take your little one out, wrap him up well. Be careful with his diet. He is not unduly bothered by food and prefers to eat little and often: he is a nibbler. Variety and change are essential. In the first months, he will want not only to taste all those lovely new dishes that you have to provide, but also to test how they feel on his fingers. Messy!

As a child grows older, he has to learn to socialise. Generally, this is not a problem for anybody from one of the Air signs. Of course, he still has to learn to share, to give and take and let others play with his toys and possessions. For a young Gemini, learning to get along with those around him can be easy, but much depends on how his overtures are met. In so many cases, he may have to learn to negotiate as well, but young Gemini has a particular flair for this. He soon learns to do it standing on his head. However, as the parent of this Air sign child, you will have to be prepared to look for the catches in the arguments put up by him. Remember, he really is a very clever little fellow.

As an older brother or sister, young Gemini makes any and all younger siblings most welcome for he will regard them as someone to nurture and guide as only he can. He enjoys the company as well. However, as a younger sibling, Gemini is inclined to be irritating and bothersome at times, to say the least.

Gemini children have excellent personal confidence levels, especially if the oldest. As a second child, he does not feel he has to outdo his fellow siblings or prove himself. He will settle into life quite readily, although Geminian boys and girls tend to flit from one idea to another as they develop. What might be considered good today is positively old hat tomorrow.

As the third child, Gemini finds it difficult to settle and learn the rules, but there is no doubt that he enjoys the challenge. When it comes to making his mark on the world, he has that happy knack of being quite resourceful and adaptable.

At school, Gemini children latch on to any teacher who captures their imagination, someone who takes the time and also has the patience to explain things to them. Through dealing with large numbers of their peers, young Geminis develop effective levels of independence or dependence quite quickly. Often, they become a law unto themselves. They will not waste time with trivia, unless it particularly captures their imagination. The Rubik cube was made for them!

Gemini children rarely make the same mistake twice because they are adaptable and learn quickly from experience as they develop their own behaviour patterns. There is absolutely no way that a young Gemini, at whatever age, could be called an introvert as he is usually so positive, open, outgoing and versatile.

6

The Cancer Child

Dates	Circa	21 June – 22 July
Ruler		The Moon
Symbol		The Crab
Metal		Silver
Colour		Blue/Greens/Violet
Part of the Body		Breasts and Stomach
Natural House		Fourth
Classification		Cardinal – Water – Negative

 Your Cancerian baby is highly unpredictable: you may never really know what to expect next. Temperamental and impressionable, the young Crab has an uncanny ability to run the entire gamut of his emotions hourly. A daily total is best left to the imagination!

Cancer is a Cardinal Water sign, indicating intuition and sensitivity. The young Crab is highly dependent, very emotional, tenacious and restless. Just about everything he does will be triggered off by his emotional responses. Once he latches on to an idea or finds a game he enjoys, he will cling to it to the bitter end.

As far as discipline is concerned, the occasional smack is all that is required to have the desired effect immediately. However, as Cancerian youngsters are such sensitive children, it is worth explaining to them the possible damaging effects of their actions otherwise they take it to heart and remember it well. If you are able to outline the consequences of his actions on other folk, he will identify with the error of his ways by thinking how he might have reacted in the same situation.

Because they frequently bottle up all this emotion, young Crabs are prone to giving way to the occasional hysterical outburst. Fortunately, they do not actually lose their tempers so much as notch up another gear on the emotional level.

The average Cancerian youngster is frequently more intelligent than most parents (or others, for that matter) realise. They are able to assimilate and retain anything that particularly appeals to them or that they consider it is necessary to learn, doing so in a very short space of time.

The most negative characteristic is their moodiness: they can be oh, so touchy. They are also born pessimists and possess an extremely wild imagination. However, provided they always have sufficient love and understanding, these children demonstrate the most delightful manners. They are so charming, constant and loyal – when *they* want!

A warm, comfortable and harmonious atmosphere is most essential for this sensitive child, who positively dislikes all unnecessary noise and discord. They also regard with particular loathing any rough-and-tumble boys' games. Most very young Crabs would rather play with a cuddly toy or invent an imaginary playmate.

The pre-school Cancerian is usually quite content to follow you around, doing the housework. A junior broom, carpet-sweeper and cooking utensils make excellent toys. Nearly all little Crabs especially love the garden.

Almost always creatures of habit, these children like to be on time and are generally easy to please. As far as food is concerned, baby Crabs will overeat if given half a chance. But if a particular dish is refused, it is most unwise to offer it again at another time or you may find that it ends up making an interesting new pattern on the wall or ceiling!

Concerning health, the young Crab is rather prone to digestive troubles because of a very sweet tooth, so keep a regular check on his weight and teeth. Keep an eye on his temperature, too. He is liable to suffer from chest problems, and the occasional wheezy or chesty cold may arise from swimming. Strangely, it would seem for children of a Water sign, that too much water is not very good for them, so don't let them overdo aquatic pursuits.

All Cancerian children mature quite young, and all develop an early sense of responsibility. However, both the boys and girls are liable to fall foul of their emotional natures, always their weakest point.

In the early days, your work will be be cut out just trying to define precisely what baby Crab's cries really mean. These babies are so impressionable that their moods are liable to change virtually at the drop of hat. All Cancerians are very dependent and extremely sensitive, traits they never lose throughout life.

Happily, most of the time your baby should be fairly content and reasonably easily pleased. However, he can also be just as easily frightened and will react quite violently if disturbed. As his eyes may follow you around the room, he will rarely make overt demands for affection. Instead, he probably just lies there, looking all pathetic, hoping for kind words, smiles or cuddles that never stop. Of course, if you weaken, you are fair game and he is in his glory.

Crabs tend to prefer little fluffy mobiles that change colour as they move in the breeze. Soft, cuddly toys are firm favourites from a very early age, and he will take good care of them. He appreciates quiet, gentle music, and dislikes anything raucous. Your choice of toys should reflect his incredibly fertile imagination so much so that you may often find he falls asleep happily under a mound of them. He will also love colourful rag-books or other soft eye-catching items.

A large play-pen with extra padding is an excellent idea, but he will also enjoy sitting in the kitchen pretending to prepare a meal and copying everything you do. He will play for hours like this. However, since he is so sensitive to everything you do, you must be very careful not to show negative emotions around him. He may be bewildered or angry and feel insecure. At a very early age, he should be made aware that people do sometimes get upset. You must make it clear to him that he should not become stressed by it. He positively hates unpleasantness.

Unfortunately for you, when it comes to sleeping, little Cancerians indulge in short naps. You will be hard put to get your own work done in the little time they allow you.

Baby Crab starts to sit up when he feels like it, often a trifle later than average in the majority of cases. In this respect, as in many others, and also because he is so emotionally orientated, he will do only what he wants when in the right mood. Fortunately, as a rule he is co-operative in most circumstances, often bending over backwards to accommodate people he likes. If you are not the flavour of the hour, forget it. It is a touch sneaky perhaps, but it pays to remember that his mother always takes precedence over everybody, no matter what.

Baby Cancerians take a little longer than average when it comes to walking and talking. He must not be rushed. However, once started be warned, for he will be up and away. He is happy to play both indoors and out, but does like to have his own little corner where he can feel free to do what he wants. Preferably this will be a sturdy but comfortable play-pen.

By six months, he will easily be able to hold toys and other articles. Like most youngsters, much of what he picks up finds its way to his mouth, so cleanliness is important.

At ten months, he should be able to stand up, initially with help, preferably from his mother. Shortly afterwards, he will start to move around and then a new phase starts. Young Cancer is a helpful, willing soul. He will even try to make his bed. On a fine day, turn him loose into the garden, remembering to keep an eye on him. If you let him, he will show all the makings of a good gardener. When a little older, allow him to have a small patch all his own – a good way to earn sainthood!

In everything he does, the Cancerian youngster moves around happily exploring all the new and unfamiliar territory at his own pace. When unsure of anything, whether people, places or things, he will exercise great caution, a typical Cancerian trait. He has a naturally shy personality and rarely changes. He can be erratic and moody, but able to switch on the charm or bare his soul with equal facility in order to get his own way.

He may have to be coaxed into talking at first, but once he does, which could be earlier than average, he soon develops a fair vocabulary. By eighteen months, his natural curiosity will have him asking all sorts of questions. And he will want answers! He needs to have explanations, to learn, to find out why: it is all part of the Cancerian approach.

All the usual safety precautions must be taken. Arrange a safety gate on the landing, and do shut doors that are meant to be kept shut. A guard-rail on top of the cooker will keep him away from the pots, pans and kettles that are so potentially dangerous.

These little Crabs are no more accident-prone than children of other signs, but do have their weaknesses in matters of health and almost always display a sweet tooth. Cancer is a Water sign, and Cancerians often retain water when sick. The stomach and the digestive system are also sensitive. Some may have eye problems, such as a lazy eye, in their early years. You must be careful with your Cancer child's diet: he likes to eat when he is ready, which more often than not tends to be before it has been prepared.

As the little Crab grows older, he has to learn to socialise and usually makes the rules of any association once he finds that not all people are like him. Sharing, learning to give and take, and letting others play with his toys and possessions are not easy for him. The art of negotiation is also learned the hard way. From early childhood through adulthood, the Cancerian will have very few really close friends, but creates a fairly wide-ranging circle of acquaintances from all walks of life.

As the eldest child, the young Cancerian looks upon his siblings as people to nurture and guide as only he can. But as a younger brother, he can feel inferior and may find it hard to keep up with a brighter, older brother or sister. He will try to learn from them, but might take quite a few knocks in the process.

Single Cancer children have lower than average levels of personal confidence. As a rule, a Cancerian second child exhibits even less confidence and is likely to turn more than is good for him to an older child for advice and guidance. He is far too trusting and easily fooled, making himself vulnerable to other children in certain cases.

As the third child, Cancer finds it difficult to settle and learn the rules. He dislikes having to battle with older brothers and sisters in order to make his presence felt in the family. While a young Crab can be quite resourceful, he is not always as adaptable as he needs to be. He finds it difficult to socialise and be compatible with his peers. To most young Crabs, anyone who is older must be wiser and respected. At school, therefore, a Cancerian child quickly latches on to any teacher who is prepared to spare the time to capture his imagination.

As he grows and learns from life's experiences, he will develop like any other child, but often seems to suffer for his pains. There is absolutely no doubt that at whatever age our young Crab is basically an introvert. Cancerians usually stay with what they know and are quite traditional in outlook. Their dislike of change means that what is good today holds just as well tomorrow. They can be rather closed personalities, not keen to adapt but surprisingly versatile when the mood takes them. They should never be under-estimated at any time!

7

The Leo Child

Dates	Circa 22 July – 22 August
Ruler	The Sun
Symbol	The Lion
Metal	Gold
Colour	Gold/Orange
Part of the Body	Heart and Back
Natural House	Fifth
Classification	Fixed – Fire – Positive

 The Leo baby has a most positive little personality and makes his presence felt immediately. Bossy and restless, with a strong imperious side to his character, a juvenile Lion will not be ignored by anyone for any reason. He automatically assumes and believes that everyone else is around just for his benefit.

Leo is a Fixed Fire sign, which denotes pride and purpose. The little Lion is hardly ever still long enough to take breath and is here, there and everywhere, dominating everything and everyone with a sense of his own importance.

Young Lions are full of fun and mischief all the time so that when it comes to discipline, parents really do have their hands full. They need to try to maintain a fine balance between keeping their child under firm control and giving him the freedom he demands. When necessary to dole out punishment, perhaps one of the best methods is to withdraw certain privileges and restrict some of his freedom. It usually does the trick. A first-class reprimand that diminishes his status is also very effective, but in order to achieve success in this area, you will first of all have to learn how to ignore your young Lion's wicked charm.

Be warned: if you fail to exercise parental authority properly, you will soon find yourself living with an arrogant, demanding, petulant, boastful and domineering little dictator who makes you despair at times. However, once you manage to win his respect, then you will find you have an ambitious, responsible, self-confident, romantic and charitable child who develops into a fine leader of men.

Young Leo enjoys company, but needs an exacting, stimulating and vital environment in which he may consistently shine. Dramatic pursuits have a great appeal for him. Unfortunately, so do noisy ones. Musical instruments, dancing and singing or any form of creative game will interest him and hopefully capture his imagination. If he can dress up, so much the better, for here his ingenuity is inexhaustible. Leo is the sign of theatre and drama. All Lions, no matter what their age, are drawn sooner or later in some way to the magic of make-believe. Juvenile Lions are no exception. Allow them free rein and they can play for hours with a few close friends or even on their own, if in the mood to do so.

When it comes to food and his diet in general, he can be very fussy and probably prefers frequent but small meals. Sometimes, he may even completely forget to have a meal. But do not worry: it is all quite normal for a little Lion. There might be a few occasions when he comes to the table and only picks at the meal, but he will devour the next one eagerly. Making a fuss over him at meal times might encourage him, but try not to force him to eat when he does not want to, for you will not win the ensuing battle if you do.

Leo children are quite resistant to the usual day-to-day childhood bugs and viruses. Their weakest points are perhaps the heart and back. It pays to look after their health carefully because a bedbound Lion tends to become very frustrated with his enforced inactivity. In the end you may be the one who really needs the doctor!

Young Leo has purpose, pride and ambition: he knows he can reach the top, even if he has to stoop to one or two underhand tricks in order to achieve his aims. He appreciates the difference between right and wrong, but it is up to you to see that he always remembers the distinction.

In the first few months, baby Leo will always let you know when your parental services are needed. His eyes will follow you and respond to any other visual stimulus almost the moment he arrives. Small or highly coloured mobiles that make a sound in the moving air please him. He enjoys all the attention he can get. Whilst not averse to little cuddles, he does not like to feel restricted, so hold him loosely but carefully.

A baby Lion is an explorer and remains that way all his life. If he feels he can get away from you, he will do so like a shot! But long before reaching that stage, he will have discovered the power of his most terrifying weapon – his voice. As soon as he is old enough to realise how readily you drop everything at his first cry, he quickly learns to use it. Despite his tender age and diminutive size, he will insist on your attention all day and every day. The little bundle of joy you brought home will within a very short space of time rule everything and everybody.

Like all babies, young Leo will sleep for about two-thirds of each day, though not in one session. He enjoys quick naps that refresh him, but are rarely quite long enough for your liking. In most cases, but not all, he should be sleeping through the night by the time he is six months old.

Active and physically adventurous from the start, by four months he will be able to sit up with the minimum of assistance from an adult. By six months, he should also be able to manipulate many of his little toys. As he usually has a reasonably developed sense of taste and smell, much of what he picks up soon finds its way to his mouth.

Baby Lions begin to move around slightly earlier than most other signs. Once mobile, you will have to be very firm with him. Leo children move very swiftly indeed, so be prepared. By eight months he ought to be able to stand up, and by nine or ten months – a little earlier in some cases – will be managing some element of real mobility.

Discipline and supervision are now very important: he needs to be taught who is the real boss and must learn to respect your authority. With a baby Lion child this is none too easy a task! It would not hurt briefly to explain why he should not touch this, but can play with that because he needs to know. It does not matter if he cannot fully understand your explanations in the beginning, but will serve to get you to remember and do it automatically until he gets the idea firmly embedded in his mind. He should be taught to respond immediately to the word 'No!' as soon as you possibly can.

Little Lions seem to manage to get everywhere and anywhere at any time. He is insatiably inquisitive and a born explorer, so once he masters movement, he is off. When he has the opportunity to move outside his normal nursery environment, he will be captivated by everything. It will all be so new to him. Anything he has not previously experienced acts as a magnet, so you must ensure that he cannot get into trouble. He may also now get quite frustrated at his own inability to do things as swiftly or as deftly as he might prefer. A temper tantrum from baby Leo is a sight to behold, but it does not normally last very long and he is soon off on his chosen path towards new discoveries once more.

The little Lion starts to talk early and should have a small but useful vocabulary by the time he is about 15 months. He quickly learns how to ask questions about everything that catches his ever-alert eye. He has a very strong need to learn, to find out 'Why' For the most part, he just enjoys the experience of satisfying his curiosity. Once this is done, he will return to his exploring ways again.

Make no mistake: little Leo is a born adventurer. Leo-proof safety measures of all kinds are absolutely essential, including gates at the top and bottom of the stairs. You will probably also want to fence off hazardous areas such as the kitchen, where his curiosity will lead him to investigate all kinds of potential dangers.

His health will generally be good, but for all Leo children the back and chest areas are among the most vulnerable parts of the body. Make sure he is not able to pull anything on top of himself. Because of their inquisitive natures, some little Leos are accident-prone whilst quite a few have very sensitive skin. In the summer time, they should not be left out in the sun for too long without adequate protection. Your little Lion cub can also be quite sensitive to the cold so when you take him outdoors wrap him up well.

Occasionally, it is not unknown for some Leo babies to develop a fever from out of nowhere. Just how and what may be the cause of the problem depends on the prevailing circumstances of the time: extremes of weather or it might be due to something he has eaten. While this is not a very pleasant episode, as long as you follow the right procedures it is soon over and he will rapidly be back to normal.

When the time comes for a Leo to learn to share and socialise, it may present more than just a few problems for them. Leo folk are rather possessive. No matter how old they are, getting along with others is not always easy until they get used to the idea of give and take in equal portions. Further, young Leo is most unhappy if put in a position where he has to negotiate: he is a leader, not a follower. He assumes he has the right to take power automatically and expects to be followed without argument. It comes as a bit of a shock to his system if things do not naturally go his way.

Single Leo children are always full of self-confidence. The arrival of younger brothers and sisters will not alter this. He considers himself to be the leader anyway: this simply strengthens his hand and resolve. He never forgets and very rarely forgives – at least that is how it may seem on the surface. Those who have opposed or stood in his way before will be remembered all the more.

As a second child, he does not feel a need to outshine his older siblings. Meanwhile, as the third child, once again young Leo is quite resourceful, although not always very adaptable. He has a rather fixed nature and does not take it lightly if and when his plans go awry.

Little Leo girls tend to have more energy than their lazier brothers. Both mature at about the same rate, but a sense of responsibility comes earlier to the females. However, all young Lions are natural extroverts. They are among the most outgoing and positive of the zodiac personalities even though they can be rather fixed in their ways. But in spite of this, they are popular and natural leaders among their peers. They learn quickly from their mistakes as they add and discard from their ever-growing fund of life's experiences.

Because they also like to take responsibility, they may become stressed when events do not go right for them. If this is allowed to get out of hand while still young, they might well carry this into adulthood, which is not a good idea. They must be taught to relax, but properly.

8
The Virgo Child

Dates	Circa 22 August – 23 September
Ruler	Mercury
Symbol	The Maiden
Metal	Quicksilver
Colour	Grey/Dark Blues
Part of the Body	Hands and Nervous System
Natural House	Sixth
Classification	Mutable – Earth – Negative

 As a rule, Virgo babies often arrive in a relatively peaceful and harmonious fashion – and do their utmost to keep it that way throughout their lives. In spite of an apparently cool approach, the majority of Virgos have rather strong personalities, but are very loving in their own special way.

Virgo is a Mutable Earth sign, suggesting service. Children born under this sign are most likely to be helpful, neat, tidy and even a little fussy, which makes discipline a basically straightforward affair. Nevertheless, although usually obedient and well-behaved, a Virgo child can sometimes play up in the most rebellious fashion for what may seem to be no apparent reason – at the time. So when he is being frustratingly irresponsible, try appealing to his logic and life ought to return to normal fairly quickly.

The main problem for these children is boredom. A young Virgo has to have all the mental stimulation he can get for he becomes mean, fretful, tactless, prudish, complaining and critical when his mind is not fully occupied.

His senses are very acute. He also has a sensitive touch. In certain cases, he may be the first to notice that something is not quite right and sound the alarm. In early childhood days, adults might ignore this. Only after it happens on several occasions do people sit up and take note. Ignore the Virgo child at your peril!

Happy Virgo is methodical, orderly and truthful. He will do well at school because of his ability to concentrate and retain information easily. He thrives best in affectionate and uncluttered surroundings that allow him complete freedom to exercise his intellectual talents. Thus, educational toys are the most suitable for this observant youngster, who probably also enjoys long leisurely walks that offer opportunities to look and learn. If he is in the mood, very little escapes his attention. Once collected, objects will rarely be discarded, for many Virgoans are fanatical hoarders.

Virgos are creatures of habit and usually prefer regular meals, although they often seem to eat very little and are frequently very choosy. In many cases, this may simply be a matter of diet. A high proportion of Virgos do not like meat very much. Just balance his diet according to his wishes and do not worry too much as he will ask for food when he is hungry.

Concerning health, young Virgoans are prone to skin disorders, stomach upsets, and any number of minor ailments. The frequency of their complaints may make them seem like junior hypochondriacs which, frankly, they could well become if given half a chance. However, as a rule they grow out of this.

A Virgo child displays a good sense of responsibility from a very early age. In later life, he will be well suited to work in a service industry because of an affinity with his fellow men and concern for their well-being.

The Virgo baby dislikes change of any sort and makes this known as soon as he arrives. Change can bring uncertainty, and young Virgo hates the insecurity this brings. He prefers a set routine and a consistent approach at all times. You will soon discover this as you have to adapt and take care of this new, dependent little soul. However, as a baby he tends to be a rather tranquil little fellow, apparently content to lie quietly in his cot. In all probability, he is sizing up the opposition – you! – so it won't take long for him to assume control despite his age and size. Routine he wants . . . and routine he will have.

He is alert at a very early age, his eyes following you around. He will also respond to other visual stimuli. He appreciates touch throughout his life and loves home comforts. In fact, nearly all little

Virgos love to wallow in comfort, so always make sure his immediate surroundings reflect this.

Baby Virgo likes attention, but might find it difficult to show his inner feelings. While it is not exactly rare for them to display their emotions in public, Virgo children are often reluctant to demonstrate acts of affection, even mildly, when greeting someone they have not seen for a while. A formal handshake will have to suffice until later. He enjoys the security your cuddles offer, but will also exhibit an independent streak from a very early age. Just hold him firmly, support him well – and he will soon tell you when he wants you to stop!

In most cases, baby Virgo establishes a good sleep routine fairly early around the norm of about 14 hours a day, including a few day-time naps. He should go through the night any time after four months or so.

As a rule, Virgos tend not to move around very much in the early stages, but have inquiring minds. By the time your child starts to move about, perhaps slightly later than the average of other children, he will be alert and aware of what is going on all around him.

As early as four to five months or so, he ought to be able to sit up if supported, and by around six months will develop a liking for things he can hold or wield in some way. In particular, toys like bricks that he can stack and books with big clear pictures he can look at appeal the most. He will try to keep his toys in an orderly fashion. Whatever he has, he will always keep clean and tidy.

With his highly developed sense of touch and smell, baby Virgo learns to test everything with his mouth, but his fastidiousness means that he won't try this with anything if there is even the the slightest doubt in his mind about its cleanliness. Because Virgo is an Earth sign, this baby is practical and likes to be actively occupied. When he gets dirty enough, he will enjoy a bath, although only up to a point. Unlike most babies, he is keener on the actual cleaning process than playing in the water.

Virgo children respond well to discipline, especially when you explain what might happen if their misdeeds are allowed to continue. However, he has plenty of common sense of his own, and is generally quite well-behaved. But be warned: if he decides to dig in his heels, little will move him. No matter how you try to shift his stance on a particular issue, he will hold fast to the bitter end.

At around eleven months, he ought to be able to stand up and begin to move around soon afterwards. He should not give too much trouble, but like other children must be taught early that some things may be touched and others avoided. He will respond to a gentle smack on his hand, but you must remember that he is sensitive and has a long memory.

Compared to some babies of other signs, your little Virgo won't present you with many difficulties in the early days. On the whole, he will stay put and be quite happy to sit for hours in one place, playing with his favourite toys. He is also patient and attentive, content to sit in his high-chair while watching you go about your daily routine, especially if you can explain what you are doing at the same time. Initially, of course, he won't understand. But as he becomes a little older and his grasp of communications improves, he will value these sessions very highly.

While relatively inquisitive, he is not inclined to explore new territory once he masters moving around. Almost all Virgo children have a streak of curiosity that you can satisfy with very simple puzzles to keep them engaged and out of mischief.

When he starts to talk, the young Virgo develops quite a broad vocabulary which he uses to ask seemingly interminable questions. He has to learn; he actually loves to learn. But he is also precise and rather selective. He can become totally absorbed with the matter to hand when in one of these moods.

Once he starts to move, it will be slowly at first, but child-proof safety gates at the top of the stairs should be installed as well as one that divides off places little Virgos must not be allowed to explore at any time. However, having made that point, it is not unknown for a young Virgo child to close a gate or a door that has been inadvertently left open. He learns very quickly: he knows he is not supposed to go through, so closes it himself!

By the time he is about two years old, a little Virgo child will be quite settled in his ways. By then he has found all the comfortable nooks and crannies into which he is allowed. When the mood suits him, he will enjoy turning them into comfortable little play areas.

The Virgo child is not greatly accident-prone, but may not always spot the dangers that surround him. You need to keep a close eye, especially when he is out in the garden, to stop him getting into hazardous situations.

He is inclined to over-eat and could experience tummy troubles. He worries about himself from day one, which can cause stress. Some Virgo children are prone to skin troubles, possibly because their diet is not well-balanced as they are so fussy about food. Unfortunately, when a Virgo child is unwell, he makes a very poor patient. For him, the discomfort is unbearable. He is also a bit of a hypochondriac, something that rarely goes away, even as an adult.

Growing older, he will start to mix with other children, a relatively easy matter for young Virgoans. As a rule, he is not too difficult to get along with, but there will be a hint of a selfish streak due to his love of order and neatness. He has a caring attitude towards his brothers or sisters and will even try to look after them at times. He expects loyalty and honesty in return.

A young Virgo adapts and compromises easily, but adds a few 'strings' to some of his dealings. A pretty shrewd operator when he wants to be.

As an only child, young Virgo has good levels of confidence that serve him equally well when he is the eldest as brothers or sisters come along. The same self-assurance is displayed by Virgo children who are second in the family. They do not seem to feel any need to try to compete with their elder siblings.

If the third child, a Virgo youngster adapts reasonably well, but must have his own clearly defined space. He is naturally sociable, but as he grows and learns what some people can really be like, tends to be rather more selective in his choice of friends.

Although a Virgo child can be fairly set in his ways, even at an early age he will show resourcefulness. As a rule, young Virgo manages to live life with his peers largely on his own terms.

At school, he will compare teachers with his parents, but does not often have a favourite, although any teacher who takes time really to explain things to him in the way he likes will receive a more favoured reception.

The Virgo child soon learns to recognise his mistakes, but all too frequently fails to avoid the same incidents happening again. It is not so much that he finds it difficult to adapt, just that he just doesn't like change. As he starts to develop his personal behaviour patterns, he may be less flexible than most. On the whole, a very young Virgo child is inclined to be a little introverted. He is rather placid and a little shy, but far from totally negative.

9
The Libra Child

Dates	Circa	23 September – 23 October
Ruler		Venus
Symbol		The Scales
Metal		Copper
Colour		Blues/Pinks
Part of the Body		Kidneys
Natural House		Seventh
Classification		Cardinal – Air – Positive

 Your new Libran son or daughter should present the traditional picture of a perfect baby: warm and cuddly, beautiful and lovable. Often noted for their looks, both sexes have winning smiles, and are always very quick to use them!

Libra is a Cardinal Air sign, which means balanced responsiveness. Libran children are not the most energetic in the world, but they might well be the most inquisitive. Their innate curiosity leads them anywhere and everywhere. They are forever seeking new and fresh experiences. Not really sporting types, they enjoy the more gentle pastimes. Nearly all are artistically gifted.

A Libran child needs carefully balanced discipline. Any attempt to use physical punishment will get you absolutely nowhere, but when you appeal to his very strong sense of justice and fair play, you will probably find that he is extremely amenable. Although he does not often misbehave or display open defiance, a young Libran can be cunning and sly. A short, sharp disciplinary object lesson is often the best course of action and usually does the trick.

Often, many Librans are unsure as to whether they prefer their own company or that of others. Although they make friends easily, they relish periods of seclusion. It is not unknown for them to withdraw completely from all other social contact for short periods in order to concentrate on re-charging their batteries, but it will be done in their way.

They need plenty of freedom and a clear, uncluttered environment to encourage them to move out of their immediate surroundings. In the strictest sense of the word, Librans find it difficult to do this. They like an ordered life, preferably with the people and things they know and trust.

Normally, they are reasonably loyal, sociable, charming and amiable, but the discontented young Libran can also be indecisive, unrealistic, lazy, insincere and display escapist tendencies. He may also be dreadfully untidy.

Ideally, a Libran child's surroundings should be colourful and warm, providing him with a place where he can relax in his own way and in privacy. Music soothes and stimulates this creative child, who prefers soft toys or simple puzzles and games that keep his mind active, alert and occupied. He also likes to play with water – until it comes to bath time, when you may find you have a fight on your hands!

Libran youngsters usually appreciate practically any food put in front of them. However, they can be fastidious. If they decide a meal is in some way unacceptable, nothing will induce them to eat it. In such cases it is a wise parent who checks it: there may actually be something wrong with it.

If your neighbour's child catches measles, little Libra will think he has it as well, for many Librans have a tendency to hypochondria and may frequently suffer from psychosomatic illnesses. Bladder, blood and kidney disorders are the most likely health hazards.

Librans are born survivors. Irrespective of their sex, they give little cause for you to worry too much about their individual futures. The Libra boy almost always seems to manage to attract a girl who will cater for his every whim while the slightly more self-sufficient Libran girl has the happy knack of turning on enough charm to melt even the hardest of hearts to get what she wants.

In the early days, you are going to have to learn to distinguish between your new baby's cries for attention and discover what each one means. As a rule, it is for the usual services. However, Libra children get bored easily and need plenty of items in and around their cots to keep them properly occupied and stimulated.

Small mobiles are a perennial favourite, perhaps best with an in-built sound as they move about in the breeze. Anything else that creates a noise suits as well, but you will have to change them around fairly regularly to create variety and change.

While baby Libra responds well to most forms of change, which he tends to regard as a stimulant, like those of the other Air signs he is insatiably curious, so his toys should reflect this. He enjoys attention and flattery from anybody who will give it – his parents, other family members, their friends and even the neighbours. Right from an early age, he loves to be with people and relishes cuddles to feel needed: just being near to someone else delights him. But do be careful for he dislikes restriction of any kind.

This little one may sleep for much longer than the average 14 to 15 hours a day which most babies seem to need. He is likely to enjoy long naps and snoozes as well. Of all the signs, Librans are natural cat-nappers.

Baby Libra will sit up when he is ready and not before, so you will be unable to force the issue. By the time he is about six months or so, he will start to grasp and handle his toys along with other play-things with ease. He particularly likes regular excursions out of doors, as long as he is tucked up and warm.

Some children are naturally solitary, will play alone for hours and not seem to worry if others are about or not. This suits baby Libra quite well. If others are present, he might sit and watch them, though if the mood takes him, he may join in. He needs a large play-pen, preferably with corners. The young Libran will then arrange each corner for a particular activity. In this respect, he may seem organised, but is nothing like a Virgo.

One day when he feels confident enough to do so, he will just stand up and begin to move and walk. He soon leaves the crawling stage behind. There may be no set programme for this. Once walking and talking, he will still spend a lot of time hidden away for long periods in one corner or another. This may be a little unnerving for his parents. Somehow you expect him to be moving around all over the place, so when he disappears and does not respond to your call it can be quite worrying at first. However, he is not being awkward, but gets so totally absorbed in what he is doing that the rest of the world has simply to carry on without him. His virtually insatiable curiosity leads him to explore to his heart's content. Too much silence might seem unnatural, but it can become a way of life with this baby.

The young Libran should begin to talk quite early, probably sooner than most of his contemporaries. He quickly acquires a wide vocabulary to make himself understood. Often, when many Librans grow up they become writers and editors. All have investigative minds and will ask all manner of searching questions. You must answer him in full at all times: he thirsts for knowledge and wants the answers with explanations as well. He learns quickly and should always be encouraged.

Baby Libra can – and will! – throw a few wobblies when something annoys him. He becomes very upset if frustrated at not being able to master a problem or if, in his view, he is subjected to any injustice or unfairness. Librans do not like to be wrong-footed in any way at any age, often laying blame anywhere but on themselves. Excuses to prove their point have to be heard to be believed. Some moodiness may be apparent, but a Libran child's fit of temper generally does not last too long. He soon comes out of it and is on his way again.

Libra likes comfort and security. He is not unduly bothered by safety gates or other ways of keeping him out of trouble because he soon recognises them for what they are. Of course, you should still install them, but if you leave one open by mistake there is no need to worry. Take the time to explain carefully about the inherent dangers and it should suffice. By the time he is about two years old, this youngster will have explored everywhere he has been allowed to go and picked up a few bumps and bruises here and there. Little Librans are no more accident-prone than other children, but have their moments. The main health problems are likely to be disorders of the blood and kidneys, and infections.

Be careful with his diet. He can be very fussy, prone to the fads and fancies of the moment. All light foods, salads and fresh fruit are best. Anything that satisfies his eternal sweet tooth is always welcome, but you must ration him. Make sure he has a varied diet with plenty of water. Learning to mix with other children is not a problem for an Air sign child. Of course, he must be taught to share, give and take, and let others play with his possessions. No matter what age, we all have to get along as best we can with those around us, but for young Libra this is relatively easy as he is naturally a sociable animal. From an early age, he readily welcomes new faces in his circle and does so all his life. However, a lot depends on how the first few minutes of any new encounter go. Once he has formed an opinion of someone, he rarely changes his mind.

Young Libra is an adept negotiator. But Libra is an Air sign, so look for the one-sidedness of any deal because in the long run it will always favour him. Librans are natural born mediators and negotiators, and are very clever indeed.

Usually, young Libra makes new arrivals in the family most welcome for he will look upon a younger relative as someone to protect and guide, and also makes a splendid bodyguard.

As a younger brother, little Libra is perfectly happy as long as everything is shared equally. If not, he is irritating, to say the least. Because he has a strong sense of justice and insists on fairness at all times, he will be quite bothersome until everything is distributed and shared out equally . . . and that means down to the last inch of space in a shared bedroom!

The single Libran child is outwardly self-confident, but finds it hard to make decisions at times. If the oldest in the family, he will demonstrate how easy it is to bluff his way with younger brothers and sisters to get what he wants.

A second Libran child tends to have a little less confidence, but makes up for this with slightly more aggression. This can show when he has to outshine fellow siblings to prove himself. Once again, young Libra will have no problems bluffing his way through. In his efforts to settle down and find a niche, most Libran boys are not quite as positive as their sisters and are often changeable as they move from one idea to another. What is acceptable now may not be so tomorrow.

As the third child, little Libra finds it a difficult position and something of a challenge, but on the whole he is equal to the task of making his mark. If he puts his mind to it, he can achieve anything he wants. Most children are quite adaptable and he soon learns to become compatible with his peers. However, there is always a lot of rivalry between brothers and sisters in any family so do make sure he is treated fairly at all times.

At school, the Libran child is likely to become emotionally and intellectually attached to any teacher who is prepared to give him extra attention. As long as he is given plenty of explanation and understands both sides of a question, he makes a willing pupil, getting along well with his peers.

Librans can be either introverts or extroverts, depending on circumstances. It seems that not only how they react to someone they are dealing with, but even the time of day may affect their behaviour. On their own, they tend to be closed personalities, but in company are companionable and responsive.

10
The Scorpio Child

Dates	Circa	23 October – 22 November
Ruler		Pluto
Symbol		The Scorpion
Metal		Iron/Plutonium
Colour		Deep Reds
Part of the Body		Sexual Organs
Natural House		Eighth
Classification		Fixed – Water – Negative

 Scorpio babies makes their presence felt from the start. They are deeply emotional, very demanding and possess the ability to change moods with astonishing speed, so much so that you may think you have a junior Jekyll and Hyde personality on your hands!

Scorpio is a Fixed Water sign, which denotes determination. These youngsters are born fighters in every respect – bouncing, vital, tough little individuals with very strong survival instincts. A young Scorpion can be a villain of the first order, but as long as you earn his respect by being firm, even ruthless if you feel it necessary, he will soon learn obedience. It is absolutely essential for a young Scorpio to feel the effects of your discipline: he must see that it is done justly. Ideally, one of the best methods is to confiscate a treasured possession for a short time. That almost always brings them up short.

Scorpios are very intense, rather secretive and usually acquire really deep-seated feelings very early. Proud and strong-willed, this child will be precocious and over-possessive unless taught otherwise at an early age. Try to encourage his resourcefulness and creative talents and you will be repaid with love, respect and undying loyalty. When you make friends with a Scorpio of any age, you create an ally for the rest of your life.

The Scorpio child has to have a quiet place where he can be on his own for short periods because privacy is important to him. In order to retain his interest, toys should be physically challenging or constructive. A cycle, xylophone, Meccano or Lego kit, pedal-car or – heaven forbid! – a drum will all meet his needs. However, be prepared to tidy up after him when he loses interest because Scorpios of any age or either sex tend to be very untidy. They abandon things where they lie. As they happily chase off after pastures new, it is down to you to collect and tidy away. An enterprising way to teach him tidiness is to put everything he leaves around into a box or cupboard. When he asks for an item, look and protest innocence. Some take slightly longer than others to get the message.

Young Scorpions have very decided tastes in all things and will not eat anything they do not like. Do not waste time in trying to force the issue or the food will end up on the floor. Scorpions eat what they want, when they want it!

Health-wise, they are solid youngsters, although nervous tension can cause upset stomachs. As a rule, both boys and girls are self-sufficient and mature very early. They also learn quickly how to look after themselves – with or without your co-operation.

In the early days, your work is going to be reasonably easy for this little one likes his sleep. While not exactly lazy, he often gives the impression of being unenthusiastic. At times, his moods are liable to change almost without any apparent cause. He is emotionally dependent and very sensitive, and tends to stay this way throughout adulthood.

Most of the time, young Scorpio is content and reasonably easily pleased. However, he can become quite violent if unable to get his own way and will resort to very extreme behaviour if he feels it necessary. He is always exceptionally determined.

In the very early days, as he watches you move around, he does not make many overt demands for much. But baby Scorpio needs to be assured he is surrounded by affection, security and comfort, though not always in that order. Then, when you least expect it, he takes over, and is suddenly the boss. If he cries for attention, he wants it immediately . . . and for as long as he wants it. He may not respond much to a cuddle, but will if he sees anyone else having one, as jealousy is a major fault in these children. Share your time with him carefully because if you fail to do so in these early days, you are fair game and he becomes something of a tyrant.

Scorpions like pastel colours and respond well to soft music. Cot toys should be reasonably strong or kept out of reach. He has an investigative mind and is liable to rip anything apart to see how it is made. Objects that keep his mind occupied or test his abilities as well as appeal to the imagination are most suitable.

A larger than usual play-pen with extra padding to allow him to bounce around is a good idea. As a baby, he will also enjoy being carried around strapped to your back – or front – in a papoose style so that he can be with you all the time.

The Scorpio child is rather complex emotionally. Take care not to give off too many negative vibes while with him as he might well sense your mood and take it on himself, without understanding why. At an early age, he needs to be taught that people of all ages do get upset and that it is perfectly normal. If he becomes stressed, he is liable to translate this into a physical response. He is so energetic, so full of vim and vigour that he might take it out on the next person or toy he meets. A young Scorpion can be quite violent when his temper shows.

Whilst many babies sleep for up to 14 hours daily, little Scorpio may indulge himself for even slightly longer. He also has a lazy streak and will enjoy extra short naps.

Baby Scorpions start to sit up when they feel like it, often much later than average. However, as this youngster can be so intense, he will do only what he wants and when he is in the mood. Often, he also starts to walk and talk later than average. Try not to be tempted to rush him: he will start in his own good time. Once he does, he will be up and away.

When he begins to talk, baby Scorpio is quickly able to put his words together, but has to be taught how to speak to people and ask for things properly. Scorpions have an annoying habit of seeming to be abrupt, but this is just their way: they mean nothing by it. His natural curiosity makes him ask all kinds of questions, but ensure you give the proper answers. Do not try to fob him off.

As a rule, young Scorpio is a most co-operative child, but if he should decide to be otherwise really can be difficult. He enjoys being the centre of attention – usually all the time.

He likes life in and out of doors, but most of all needs to feel free to do what he wants in his own little corner or in his play-pen. From about six months, he should be able to hold and manipulate firmly. Of course, much of what he picks up finds its way to his mouth so it is very important to keep his play area clean.

By 11 months or so, he ought to be able to stand up, but may not bother to do so until after his first birthday. Once on the move, a whole new adventure begins. It is essential you take all the usual safety precautions because he is particularly good at finding weak spots in objects as well as people. He will totter back to you bearing such a variety of interesting trophies you would not have thought it possible!

All normal safety measures – gates on landings and child-proof barriers that are supposed to keep him from danger – are for children of other signs and not a Scorpio. Be warned: when his investigative streak takes over, anything new, unfamiliar and dangerous acts like a magnet. He will be fascinated by anything he has not seen before and can spend hours playing with his finds. A Scorpio lad is just as interested in guns and other weaponry as with soft cuddly toys. He is also likely to dress up and play 'Let's pretend' when the mood takes him.

Scorpions are a little accident-prone, but you should not worry about this for it rarely involves anything very serious. However, his digestive system tends to very sensitive so if he complains of tummy ache, do take it seriously. When he mentions strange aches and pains, it is well to investigate because it generally takes a lot to upset a young Scorpio. Neither boys nor girls make very good patients!

As Scorpio grows older, teach him to socialise properly for he is inclined to be possessive and tries to rule the roost. Sharing and letting others play with his toys and possessions do not come easily to him. This means learning new skills, including having to give and take, and negotiate. He will also discover the value of friendship. It must be said that once he has made a new friend, little Scorpio is very loyal and usually remains so through thick and thin. He might not have a large number of real friends, but those he does have will enjoy a particularly close and loyal relationship with him.

When a new brother or sister comes into the family, he or she is not always well received by the little Scorpion, who will be very suspicious. Eventually, however, a newcomer is made welcome, for the Scorpio child looks upon the younger relation as someone to

67

guide as only he can. If a younger brother himself, young Scorpio does not allow older siblings to treat him as an inferior. He will always hold his own, no matter how hard things might be.

Single Scorpio children usually have good levels of personal confidence. As a parent, you will find out just how much if you ever find yourself having any sort of confrontation with him. As a rule, a Scorpio second child needs more confidence than most and will turn to older children for advice, but is inclined to be a little too trusting and easily fooled. If this happens, once he realises the true situation, his erstwhile mentor soon learns the error of his ways.

As second children, Scorpios do not settle at all easily into a niche and are forever fighting for something. When a third child, Scorpio has problems and finds it difficult to adjust to this position in the pecking order. He succeeds, however, when it suits him and can usually hold his own with siblings. Unfortunately, he is also sneaky. If any rivalry between his brothers gets out of hand, he will remedy the situation his way!

Young Scorpions are usually quite resourceful and soon find the way to make up for any difference. Unfortunately, he is not very ready to adapt. In fact, he can be stubborn and fixed in his ways. His flair for stating the obvious could be disconcerting to those who hardly know him. He will extend the hand of friendship to others in genuine need and who show some semblance of helping themselves, but does not take kindly to people who always seem to talk a lot about nothing in particular. The Scorpion dislikes these chatterboxes and those who try to probe too closely. To his peers that may seem threatening, but it is rare for him to lose arguments or be on the defensive for long. Getting on with other people tends to be rather a one-sided process in a young Scorpio.

At school, the Scorpio child appreciates the teacher who makes the effort to explain carefully anything he does not fully understand. Anyone prepared to spare the time to capture his imagination is treated with respect. Young Scorpio can – and does – find life hard at times, something which may well continue into adult life. Basically, his is a rather closed personality, not that adaptable but versatile only if it suits at the time. In short, he should never be underestimated!

11

The Sagittarius Child

Dates	Circa 22 November – 21 December
Ruler	Jupiter
Symbol	The Archer
Metal	Tin
Colour	Purple/Dark Blues
Part of the Body	Hips, Thighs and Liver
Natural House	Ninth
Classification	Mutable – Fire – Positive

 The Sagittarian baby is a very active child, as every mum quickly finds out. In fact, both parents of these gregarious children will be kept constantly on the go from the day he is brought home.

Sagittarius is a Mutable Fire sign, which indicates both mental and physical activity. It might be advisable to invest in a ball and chain or at least a pair of handcuffs for your child as all little Archers are born explorers and investigators from the time they master movement.

Sagittarians of all ages are always open, friendly souls who are at their best in company. Maintaining discipline often proves difficult because while young Archers tend to stick to the rules, you may well find they wrote them in the first place! Shouting or smacking him does no good at all for he is likely to shout and smack right back. A Sagittarian child needs to have the consequences of his actions properly explained in order to appreciate the need for discipline. You must take time to do this as it will help to earn his respect and for him to acknowledge your authority.

Little Sagittarians always need lots of room to express to themselves. As a rule, they are attracted to all kinds of sports, but in their quieter moments these boisterous, agile youngsters will also enjoy playing with puzzles or musical instruments. Extremely restless, your little Archer may be tactless, reckless, unreliable, disloyal and selfish if his mind is not kept fully occupied. It is therefore in both your interests to keep him as busy and happy as you can, but you must not pander to or spoil him. When you succeed in achieving this magic balancing act, you will be delighted with your practical, imaginative, generous and honest offspring.

As a small child, he makes sure you stay on a constant red alert because apart from being a natural escape artist, this inquisitive little one will open all your cupboards and drawers, and then spend hours mixing their contents. Further, you will be kept busy answering his endless questions about how things work.

There should not be too much trouble at meal-times because a young Archer's tastes are fairly wide-ranging. He tends to eat almost anything at any time. And when he is not actually eating, he will continually ask all manner of questions. You must be able to explain why he has to eat, what is happening inside him when he does, and so on. That should make meal-times educational (and probably also very entertaining for you both).

Sagittarian boys seem to have very little sense of responsibility, but curiously often become absolute pillars of society in the latter half of their lives. Sagittarian girls have similar tendencies, but invariably mature a lot earlier. They also seem to forget what they were like when young because on reaching middle age they also become highly respected citizens.

The Sagittarian is intellectual and clever. He knows he has talent and can reach the top, but will do it his way – and only when he is ready. He appreciates the difference between right and wrong, but likes to have the freedom to act as he wishes. However, to keep him on the right path, it is necessary to steer him in the correct direction from an early age.

As a baby, he has other ambitions to fulfil. For a start, he has to train you to keep him in the style to which he wants to become accustomed. At his best when busy, you will both gain much from your relationship in its early stage. He loves company and is never happier than when other folk are about: he can even fall asleep in a room full of people because that is where he feels he belongs.

The young Archer is not averse to cuddles, and revels in it when you take him out to play. It is necessary to give him all the attention he feels he so richly deserves because in later life he may have trouble in his emotional relationships. The earlier he appreciates the emotional side of life, the better. Sagittarius is not called the bachelor sign for nothing.

When left in his cot, make sure there are several small, bright mobiles that make a sound in the moving air to please him. Even as a baby, he should not be restricted too much, for the young Sagittarian is a natural explorer. If he manages to get away, he will be straight off! His love of activity starts now and remains with him all his life.

Whatever the average time for a baby to start anything new, expect your young Archer to do it much earlier. Where most babies are supposed to sleep for about two-thirds of each day, this one will often do so for much less. However, he needs his sleep because of all his hyperactive play time. He will learn to handle and manipulate small playthings at quite an early age. True to fashion and like most babies, much of what he picks up will find its way to his mouth. With a baby Archer around the house, you will have to put keeping the place clean at the top of your list of household chores.

By around five months, he should sit up with the minimum of help. He will also try to stand up early. Once he does, perhaps with a little help, some element of mobility follows shortly afterwards. When starting to move around, you will discover that Sagittarius children do so very swiftly indeed, so prepare to be firm from the start. He will have to be taught the difference between right and wrong as early as you can, but exerting any kind of authority over young Sagittarians is not always a simple task.

Like any other extremely active child, he must learn that some things may be touched while others are out of bounds. If he is not to get himself into trouble, he has to respond immediately on hearing the word 'No!'

Once starting to talk, he soon gathers a good vocabulary, but tends to ask all the right questions at all the wrong times. He wants to learn and find out why and requires an answer with a proper explanation to satisfy his curiosity.

This baby will be everywhere and anywhere at all times. If he moves outside his normal nursery environment, you must see to it that he cannot get into trouble with all the adult paraphernalia probably lying around within his reach. He is inquisitive, born to explore and so endlessly curious. He will even try climbing, if necessary, to get his hands on things he can see glittering just beyond his reach. Make no mistake: the little Archer is at risk as long as he is on the loose. He needs constant supervision, especially as all the safety gates in the world will not stop him once he makes his mind where he is going.

This child will horrify you as he experiments climbing the stairs outside the banister rail if given the opportunity! In view of this, you must put up all the barriers you can to keep him away from hazards in the home. Try not to leave anything that can tantalise him. Objects of desire that attract from any shelf or are not quite properly tucked into a drawer act as magnets. If he can see it and is sufficiently drawn, he will get at it for further investigation!

Young Sagittarians have very nasty tempers, and can be vindictive and unsympathetic. An Archer's display of temper is the stuff of legends. Fortunately, it does not last very long. He does not respond at all well to discipline either: should you shout at him, he may well shout back. Smack him and he is just as likely to smack you in return. Not very nice at all.

Instead, a better approach is to appeal to his sense of fair play and reason. This usually creates the desired response as the Sagittarian has a strong sense of justice. When all else fails, experiment by withdrawing for a while some or all of those privileges he prizes so much. For example, when deprived of freedom, he soon comes back to his senses. Any form of restriction is total anathema to him.

The young Archer is basically a healthy child, although he can experience minor digestive ailments. However, he is often clumsy and certainly accident-prone. Keep a wary eye open for the many kinds of mishaps that can befall any child who fails to look before he leaps. Watch out for bumps and bruises, and even an occasional fracture. Junior Archers rarely walk anywhere – they always run. Many get liverish, something that occurs quite regularly as they grow older. Occasional nervous complaints or psychological upsets can also arise because in certain circumstances this child is inwardly a born worrier. Not sturdy like a Taurus or Scorpio subject, he is more like a greyhound that operates best in short, sharp bursts.

Socialising and mixing with other children is a relatively easy matter for a young Sagittarian. He is constantly ready to share, and gives and takes with the best. The Archer is such a natural in competitive games and sports. All these activities bring him encounters with lots of new friends, all of whom he will always get on with quite well.

When a new member of the family arrives, at first young Sagittarius hardly notices. But when the newcomer is old enough to share in his more physical activities, this relationship will take off. Until then, he just pays lip service to it or barely acknowledges the toddler.

Most single Sagittarian youngsters have plenty of self-confidence. This will be enhanced when other brothers and sisters come along, but he must not be pressured into accepting a new baby.

As he develops his relationships with friends and family, young Sagittarius learns to negotiate, again without much difficulty because he is a natural leader, not a follower. He is liable to assume this position automatically, seeing it as his right. As a second child, he has no problem and does not feel the need to prove himself since he will just attach himself to the older child for as long as suits him.

If allowed, the Sagittarian second child easily slips into the family hierarchy, finds his niche and settles down. Boys tend to be slower and somewhat lazier than the girls at this stage, but in later life usually make solid and successful citizens.

As a third child, a young Archer learns very quickly indeed. It is a position that suits his overall approach to life. There is always rivalry between brothers and sisters, and the more there are, the better it suits him. He can – and does – play one off against the other to his heart's content. Young Sagittarius is very resourceful and adaptable in such situations.

The Sagittarian child seldom makes the same mistake twice. He is adept at using his growing fund of experience and quickly discards any information he does not need. At school, he rapidly makes friends and, given time, establishes good relations with most of his new playmates. The sheer number of children suits him perfectly. He is positive and enthusiastic, very much a social animal who soon acquires a good level of independence. Most young Sagittarius have a particularly outgoing and expansive personality. His easy-going nature will always make him very popular among peers – at any age.

12

The Capricorn Child

Dates	Circa	21 December – 20 January
Ruler		Saturn
Symbol		The Goat
Metal		Lead
Colour		Dark Greens/Browns
Part of the Body		Bone Structure and Knees
Natural House		Tenth
Classification		Cardinal – Earth – Negative

 The Capricorn baby is a relatively quiet child and always seems to appear to have a rather serious nature from childhood. He will remain so all the way through to old age.

Capricorn is a Cardinal Earth sign. This indicates practicality and determination. These youngsters nearly always give a good impression of being self-confident and strong-willed. They tend to display such a laid-back and sober attitude that it can take some adults by surprise.

Imposing discipline rarely presents a problem with the Goat, especially if you treat him like a young adult rather than as a naughty child. He likes to feel grown-up and wants to be regarded that way. Little Capricorns are usually well-behaved, so should he become sulky or rebellious there is invariably a very good reason, but you may need great patience to get to the root of the problem. The parents of very young Goats are inclined to check on them more than is necessary because they are generally so good and quiet. However, you do not really have to worry: this quiet little soul is quite content to sit in his play-pen or corner playing with toys.

Little Goats like routine and traditional play-things. They often show a surprising tidiness with all their possessions. But they do not always appreciate you clearing up after them. They have a place for everything and everything has its place.

Persistent and determined, the Capricorn youngster has an ability to absorb everything going on around him. He will also decide fairly early what really interests him and what does not. This little one is not keen on mountains of food. Instead, he is likely to nibble little and often. As long as his diet is kept well-balanced and contains all the nutrients he requires, there is no need to worry about this preference for quick snacks as they certainly won't harm him. You will have to teach him how to eat properly, or more slowly perhaps, because the Capricorn child tends to bolt his food.

As far as health is concerned, he is prone to catch colds or any bug going the rounds. Generally, the little Capricornian is inclined to be rather sickly when small, but as he grows becomes quite hardy and sturdy. In the meantime, do make sure you wrap him up well when necessary.

Other weaknesses are skin problems and, in many cases, rheumatism or other bone or sinew-related ills. A child of this group has a worrying tendency to break bones rather easily. He can also suffer from wind and flatulence because of his eating habits.

Capricorn boys are always very sensible, responsive and prepared to work to reach the top. The girls are much the same, but a little more reserved, sure and patient. They both make excellent partners, in marriage and business.

Capricorn babies tend to arrive in relative peace and harmony, and try to keep matters that way throughout their lives. The baby Goat has a very strong personality and is extremely loving in his own special way. Although usually obedient and well-behaved, young Capricorn can sometimes demonstrate a rebellious and stubborn side to his nature for no immediately apparent reason. When this happens, appeal to his logic. If you tackle the problem correctly, it will bring him back to his senses very quickly.

Once he starts to move, he tends to do so at his own pace and is still likely to be very quiet. In most cases, the Capricorn child follows the normal pattern and timescale of development, or is possibly a little slower. While he does not always move around too much, he will certainly show what an alert mind he has. Having begun moving, perhaps a touch later than might be expected, this little one quickly demonstrates that he is much more aware of what is going on than you might credit. It does not take him too long to recognise members of his family, whom he greets with a big smile.

Little Goats always thrive best in an affectionate and uncluttered environment that allows him the freedom to exercise his intellectual talents. For this reason, educational toys are particularly appreciated. At about six months, he shows his preference and liking for those he is able to manipulate or use in some way. He will play with bricks or other similar toys that he can stack or arrange in patterns as he wants. The young Goat enjoys books with big, bright pictures or those that open up to display three-dimensional illustrations he can look at. One blessing is that he will keep his toys neat and tidy, ensuring that other possessions are clean.

Although he may have a reasonably well-developed sense of touch and smell, baby Capricorn does not always test everything with his mouth. He probably does so initially, but will be so fastidious about personal cleanliness that this is not likely to last.

Capricorn is an Earth sign, which means this baby is practical and likes to do things. When he gets dirty enough for a bath, he should be washed or bathed on his own, not in company with another child, unless it is his twin. While still quite young, he is a very private individual, selective and a tad selfish. He adores water. Once in it, he is comfortable and relaxed, but only because he is being cleaned. Water is not his element.

Young Goats are usually very responsive to discipline. If doing something wrong, he will probably have already worked out the degree of punishment due long before you catch him. He dislikes unfairness, but appreciates justice. It is perfectly possible he will deliver a reasoned and balanced explanation or simply admit his guilt. Fight that!

He may not stand up until well after his first birthday and only then will he begin to move around. The young Goat develops slowly but surely. Once he starts, he will be a toucher. You will have to teach him early – and very firmly – that some things may be touched, others avoided. He won't take too kindly to a gentle smack because he is very sensitive, and also has a long memory.

Because he is so inquisitive, the young Capricorn explores any and all new areas in order to satisfy his curiosity streak. He starts a little slowly, but you should install all manner of child-proof safety fixtures and fittings as, or just before, he really gets going. No matter how powerful his exploring talents are, he is likely to stop at the first real hurdle. He is not really a climber and won't face up to the challenge.

At about two years old, perhaps a little earlier in some cases, young Capricorn should be reasonably settled and will have found several comfortable nooks and crannies where he plays as and when the mood suits him.

He is not exactly accident-prone, but might not always see the danger for himself. If he has a fall, always check for broken bones, just in case. When let loose in the garden, he may inadvertently put alien matter in his mouth, but only because his hands and fingers are dirty.

Once he starts to talk, he will probably take time to create a vocabulary to satisfy his desire for learning. He tends to be very selective and precise. It is best to speak to him as you would to another adult, but in simple terms he can understand. As a child grows older, he must learn to socialise. This is not always an easy task for young Capricorn. It takes time for him to accept or get used to new friends. He dislikes change of any kind and prefers his own company. He tends to play on his own perhaps a little more than is good for him. This is partly because he is a naturally solitary soul, one unable or unwilling to make friends as others might.

The young Capricorn does not trust others too readily and might even seem positively anti-social on occasions. If invited to attend a party, he will do everything he can to avoid it. As a very young child, he can be much happier with one or two close and trusted friends than be in a large circle of acquaintances. Strangely enough, he will feel very hurt should they leave him out of anything in favour of another activity. But that really is his own fault. As he matures, this problem eases somewhat.

From other members of the family, he is likely to insist on or demand loyalty and honesty. He may show a caring and considerate attitude towards older brothers or sisters, but will look out for younger siblings only if he feels it is required of him.

In dealings with others, Capricorn is slow to adapt and not very good at compromise. If he has little choice, he will do his best, but there may be a few strings to some of his deals.

As an only child, young Capricorn is at his most comfortable: there is no one to boss him and no one for him to have to worry about in return. He might seem confident, but can also bluff well.

Generally speaking, as a second child young Capricorn tends to exhibit even less confidence, but might display slightly more aggression. Usually, this will be when he has to outshine an older brother to prove himself. If allowed, a second child quickly finds a comfortable, settled niche.

As a third child, a Capricorn youngster is slow to adapt. He does reasonably well in the circumstances, but needs a clearly defined space for himself. He is not really a social animal at all. After discovering what some people can be like, he will probably opt out of the relationship. He is very selective in his choice of friends.

The number three child has to work very hard to make his mark. A young Goat has all the effort and energy he needs for this, but is quite set in his ways, even at an early age. If he is going to display any degree of compatibility, as a rule it will be on his terms. He is not that easy to get along with.

Once at school, he appreciates practical help to move his studies along so it is helpful if teachers realise this. He has his own pace. This is not as competitive or as fast as his contemporaries. However, he is ambitious, steady and reliable. When he does achieve his aim, you will not be able to fault him.

The sheer weight of numbers of all the other children can be an inhibitive factor in these formative years. Young Capricorn is not a bully, but may resort to similar tactics to make people leave him alone. But rest assured: he will not allow others to bully him either! He nearly always learns from past mistakes and rarely, if ever, makes the same one twice. He does not like change of any kind, and does so dislike having to adapt to new circumstances. As he begins to develop and mature, he may well prove to be less flexible than most.

A very young Capricorn child might appear introverted or seem a little shy, but he is far from totally negative. In later years, he tends to hide his light under a bushel.

13

The Aquarius Child

Dates	Circa 20 January – 18 February
Ruler	Uranus
Symbol	Water Carrier
Metal	Uranium
Colour	Bright Blue
Part of the Body	Calves, Shins and Ankles
Natural House	Eleventh
Classification	Fixed – Air – Positive

Your Aquarian baby may have given trouble before he was born, but now he has arrived you simply won't know how to handle him!

Aquarius is a Fixed Air sign, pointing towards inventiveness and communication. Always mentally alert, these junior Aquarians like to approach everything with such honesty and directness that at times it could strike absolute terror into your heart. Of all the signs of the zodiac, Aquarius is the one that conforms the least.

Discipline will be difficult to apply, for these youngsters can be disarmingly charming and eccentrically wayward. Highly inventive, although usually truthful, the Aquarian requires strong guidance in order to learn organisation and real common sense. You will need the patience of a saint to keep him out of trouble.

Aquarians are non-conformist at any age. Endearing individualists, they dislike routine and will investigate anything and everything right from the word go. On Monday he will play with his bricks; on Tuesday he may help with the housework while Wednesday will be given over to trying something new for himself. But heaven help you if you cannot find the bricks again on Thursday. And you won't like Fridays, either.

A comfortable, preferably modern environment that allows as much freedom as possible is ideal for the young Aquarian. If he can have plenty of places to explore as well, so much the better. You will need to be very careful, though: even when only a toddler and still in his play-pen, this young chap is a born escape artist. A secure harness and reins are essential when out walking, otherwise he will be off the moment your back is turned.

Young Aquarians are easy to cater for as they will probably try almost any type of food, but if yours takes a dislike to one particular item, nothing will induce him to try even a mouthful. It is possible that he will take in a lot of liquids and prefers to snack rather than sit down to formal meals. It may, therefore, take a long time to train him into acceptable meal-time routines.

Aquarian boys become a law unto themselves at a very early age. If they secretly wish for well-ordered lives, they rarely seem to enjoy one. The girls are not greatly different, but have a happy knack of finding a suitably satisfying occupation when they become adults.

In the very early days, you will have your work cut out trying to understand from his cries for attention precisely what it is that your new baby wants. Unfortunately, there is no set answer. In the initial stages at least, you may be sure that he is demanding the usual services – but that is where it ends.

The Aquarian child is perverse, difficult and awkward to try to understand at any age. He gets bored very easily and needs a lot to keep his fertile little mind fully occupied. You will find that hanging plenty of small mobiles – preferably colourful and noisy – around his cot help to distract him as they move about, but swop them around or substitute others quite frequently. All Air sign children have an insatiable streak of curiosity so your choice of toys should reflect this.

The Aquarian child has a great need for constant change to keep his little mind from stagnating. He enjoys attention and will demand it from anyone prepared to give it. As a baby, he delights in just being near to someone, but it won't last. While he succumbs to the restriction of a cuddle, he does not really enjoy it.

The Aquarian child needs more sleep than others. If woken before he has had enough, he may well have a nap or two later on. This is good since the longer he is awake, the more temperamental he becomes. Although he will enjoy a cat-nap, he does not like to miss anything.

Physical progress may well go in fits and starts. Often, a baby Aquarian will suddenly sit up as if he has been doing it all his short life. Overnight, it seems, he will master holding his toys and other objects with ease. Then, one day he just stands up and begins to walk and move around in much the same manner. Soon after he starts to walk and talk, he will select a favourite corner and play there quietly for long periods at a time, totally absorbed with what interests him. Such behaviour in a toddler may be unsettling, but you will get used to it.

Some children like to be on their own, will play alone for hours and not seem to worry if others are about or not. It is typical of the Aquarian child, who is likely to carry on as if he were still alone even if another child is in his play-pen with him. He is not being awkward, but simply so totally absorbed with what he is doing that the rest of the world must carry on without him.

Your Aquarian child will learn to talk early – generally sooner than most – and start to acquire a wide vocabulary to make himself understood. He has a searching mind and will ask many questions on all sorts of subjects. Give him proper answers with full explanations and encourage him at all times.

Aquarian children are not really receptive to discipline at the best of times and throw a wobbly when something frustrates them. They resist anything that smacks of injustice.

These youngsters can display a rebellious streak that has to be seen to be believed. They are stubborn, perverse and awkward, but also practical. If you appeal to their logic, you may find yourself negotiating terms for their punishment. Should you insist on curtailing their freedom, you had better mean what you say, for this really hurts. If possible, he will try to talk you out of it – and can be very persuasive!

The Aquarian cherishes home comforts: he likes to feel safe and secure. He does not resent your use of safety gates or other ways of penning him in. If you leave one open by mistake, there is little to worry about: he may or may not go through it as the mood takes him. Take time to explain the dangers and he will under-stand. But be warned: should young Aquarius feel so inclined, he will scale anything to get what he wants. By the time he is about two years old, he will have been all over the house and picked up a few scars on the way. He is not accident-prone as such, but has his moments.

Normally, his health is likely to be generally all right. Aquarians are in quite good shape, but tend to suffer from circulatory problems, so hardening of the veins and arteries is possible. Your child may also have a weak bone structure and suffer fractures through sheer carelessness.

Be careful with his diet. He can be very fussy and could for no apparent reason give up meat one week and dairy products the next. However, as a rule, light foods, salads and fresh fruit are always welcome. If he should decide he is off a particular sort of food, sneak in a vitamin supplement to balance his diet – he will not usually be clever enough to notice!

As he grows older, your Aquarian offspring has to learn to socialise with others, but this is an easy matter for any Air sign child. Of course, he has to learn to share, give and take, and allow others to play with his possessions, but it is unlikely to be a problem to him. He is not possessive, provided he does not want a particular item: anyone else can have it or use it. But when he desires something, you may be sure he will get it!

The Aquarian child is naturally sociable, but can be a little fixed in his views. He will welcome new faces into his circle of acquaintances, but like other Air signs his long-term acceptance of a friend depends very much on the first few minutes of their meeting. If things go wrong at that time, the association may never get off the ground. And once he has decided on an opinion or a course of action, the Aquarian rarely changes his mind.

Compatibility obviously starts in the home environment at a very early age. Here, perhaps more than anywhere, children are either taught or soon discover for themselves the delicate art of getting along with others. In many cases, this means learning to negotiate. A young Aquarian is open and friendly, but likes to give others the benefit of his often original and rather intriguing ideas. If other children do not always understand, they may well choose to leave him alone. However, if they do accept him, they quickly recognise that he has useful leadership qualities.

When needed, he may well become their spokesman. An Aquarian will thrive on this, for he knows how to negotiate. In the long run, this favours him. Of course, many factors have to be taken into account. One very important aspect is the position of the child in the family. When there is a brother or sister, the Aquarian child simply either accepts them or not. He can work or play with them as he wants.

As a younger sibling, little Aquarians are perfectly happy for as long as everything is shared equally. If not, they switch off and go and do their own thing. They will accept a properly balanced share of a bedroom, but would settle for the box-room instead. These early domestic circumstances always have a bearing on the way a child learns to adapt. The attitudes and general behaviour patterns that he starts to develop now will eventually be carried forward into adult life, moderated slightly here and there as he matures.

The single Aquarian child always seems to be self-confident and can bluff with the best of them. When younger brothers or sisters come along, he will show you how easy it is to manoeuvre to get what he wants. As a second child, the Aquarian has slightly less confidence, but makes up for this with a little more aggression. This comes to the fore when he has to outshine his fellow siblings to prove himself. Here, he will often resort to bluff to gain his own way, a built-in second nature.

If allowed, the second child soon finds his niche, but of the sexes, Aquarian girls are far more positive and settle better as a second sibling. As the third child, our Aquarian youngster enjoys the challenge. He always has a few tricks up his sleeve and copes quite well with any rivalry with brothers and sisters as long as he is treated equally at all times. All 'number three' children have to work hard to make their mark on the world, but the Aquarian child is equal to it.

When he puts his mind to it, he can achieve anything he wants. He is reasonably adaptable and soon learns how to deal with his peers. Once he starts school, you should make his teachers aware of the way his mind works so they can then use their skills to hone his. With this kind of co-operation, he will become a good pupil and get along well with both teachers and peers. Much of this depends on whether the child is an introvert or an extrovert. Aquarians belong to neither group in the real sense.

They are open and friendly, but can be cranky if pushed too far. Aquarians select friends carefully and are quite self-sufficient until involved in an emotional relationship. Then their loyalties can become quite strained.

14

The Pisces Child

Dates	Circa	18 February – 21 March
Ruler		Neptune
Symbol		Fish
Metal		Tin
Colour		Sea Green
Part of the Body		The Feet
Natural House		Twelfth
Classification		Mutable – Water – Negative

 The Pisces baby usually comes into this world with a lot of fuss, after which he sets out to create a whole lot more! Right from the start, he is able to charm you into compliance with whatever he wants with an angelic little smile and a gurgle. And make no mistake, you will fall, hook, line and sinker.

Pisces is a Mutable Water sign, which means impressionability and sensitivity. This child is highly imaginative, a dreamer and far more intelligent than most may credit, but this might not always be immediately apparent. Of all of the signs, Pisces often proves the most difficult to get to know properly or intimately.

Pisces children rarely become bored because of their incredible imaginative powers. They can play for hours with just the most basic of toys and, while doing so, tend to get totally absorbed. Your young Fish may not always hear your summons on the first call – or the second or third. You must learn to allow for this total preoccupation from the very beginning.

Discipline is easy if you use the right approach because the Pisces child is rarely downright naughty, a point you should bear in mind at all times. Always appeal to his emotional instincts and explain the possible end result of any bad behaviour, for he will appreciate the situation very quickly. Try a light smack on the hand only if all else fails.

Young Fish love to dress up. Music always appeals whilst television provides a unique magical world for such highly impressionable youngsters, but only for limited periods, please. Toys should be chosen not so much for durability, but for their ability to be utilised in hundreds of different ways.

Little Fish are not too good at long periods of concentration so it might be helpful if they have the odd toy that makes them stop and think. Intelligent, highly sensitive and basically shy, Pisces youngsters thrive in warm soft, colourful surroundings.

As far as food is concerned, tastes match like their moods – changeable. What they enjoy today may well be rejected tomorrow. Meal-times can prove exasperating, and you will need to establish a routine as early as possible. Baby Pisces is inclined to nibble little and often, but probably eat almost anything if you monitor him properly.

The health of these youngsters is often as sensitive as their personality. They do not always seem to have a very strong resistance to disease. Pisces rules the feet. Should anything affect them take early prompt action. There is also a slight chance of chest or nervous ailments, such as tummy upsets and allergies. As a rule, the Pisces youngster seems frail, but is much tougher than he looks. Their principal weakness is indulgence: they can – and often – push themselves too far if in the right (or wrong?) mood.

Both sexes are rather indecisive, although the girls are inclined to display a tough streak when really challenged. A Pisces child must have very firm guidance from the beginning or will not develop his full potential.

In the early days, baby Pisces may seem so doll-like and fragile that you tend to be too careful and in danger of mollycoddling him. Fear not: he is a lot tougher than you may believe. And he knows that so has you right where he wants! On the down side, he can be moody, impressionable and changeable, extremely dependent and very sensitive, traits he will have all his life.

Most of the time, this baby will be content and easily pleased, but might be frightened by a sudden noise or movement. Be careful not to display any negative emotions while he is with you, for he could become bewildered and feel insecure. He is always sensitive to unpleasantness of any kind, so as soon as possible teach him that while people can sometimes get upset, this is not something he should worry about.

Baby Pisces is very responsive to music, provided it is quiet and tuneful, and also attracted to sound and colour. Arrange little mobiles that change colour and make a noise as they move above his cot. Later on, he will like chiming toys, mini-musical instruments and music boxes – any kind of toy that makes a pleasant sound. More musicians come from this sign than any other so allow him full rein if he shows interest in any particular instrument or sound.

Soft and cuddly, fluffy toys also become firm favourites. Toys that exercise his vivid imagination are good for him. When he has finished with them, he will happily fall asleep beneath them.

His play-pen should be well padded with a soft floor because provided he feels comfortable, he will play for hours. He may also like to sit in his high chair as long as he can hold on to a toy or something he can play with. He will enjoy being with you when you go about your daily routine.

Like all babies, little Fish will sleep for around 14 to 15 hours a day, including a number of little naps here and there, so you may have to arrange your chores around these moments of brief respite. Baby Fish often dreams a lot. Just occasionally, he may suddenly wake crying. Do not worry too much. Soothe him gently and he will quickly get over it.

Little Fish often starts to talk before he begins to walk. He may do this a touch later than most, but because he is so imaginative, there is no need to doubt his intelligence! In the early stages, he might use the sound of something to describe what he wants rather than saying the name, but this soon stops.

He loves the comfort of being warm and indoors. In his opinion, outdoors is fine and stimulating, but not for him. His personal space is precious and he likes to feel free to play in his own little world. However, on a warm day, take his play-pen into the garden and let him discover a whole new world for his imagination to grasp. Much later on he could probably cultivate green fingers and with all your encouragement might develop the makings of a good gardener. Should you let him have his own patch once he is a little older, he will be very happy indeed.

Baby Pisces begins to move around very warily, exploring all the unfamiliar places at his own pace. What he does not know, he doesn't like, so is very careful when unsure of surroundings. This attitude applies to people, places or objects. He is naturally shy and rarely changes in this respect. Within six months or so, he should be able easily to manipulate toys, but as with so many other youngsters, much of what he picks up can soon find its way into his mouth. It really goes without saying, but keep things clean.

Once he stands up and starts to move around, the next phase begins. Naturally, all the usual safety precautions will have to be taken before he does begin to wander. Install a safety gate upstairs on the landing and at the bottom of the stairs. Fix guard rails around any hazardous appliances, especially in the kitchen.

Pisces is a Water sign, so your little Fish will be inclined to suffer many minor irritations as well as all the normal childhood ills. The Pisces child can often fall prey to allergies. Because he is so sensitive, his digestive system can easily be upset. He is also prone to colds and 'flu. However, be warned: unless seriously ill, he will try to make the most of the situation because of the attention he receives. He could remain 'sick' long after he has recovered, especially if he feels he can swing it. Also, be very careful with any over-the-counter medication: he may not need the full suggested dosage and often responds to only half of what is prescribed.

As this little Fish grows older, he has to learn to socialise, but this is not an easy business for him. He is very sensitive, inclined to seek out only those with whom he feels comfortable. At first, he may not let others play with his toys and possessions until sure they will be treated with respect. Learning to negotiate can be a difficult lesson for this young chap.

He instinctively dislikes all loud bullying types and will go to great lengths to avoid them. He makes very few real friends, but those who do get close remain so for life.

New brothers and sisters will be made welcome by the little Fish, but a genuinely warm relationship between them is not guaranteed. It will either happen or it won't. He is likely to regard looking after a younger relative as a chore. As a younger brother himself, young Pisces may feel inferior and find it hard to keep up. He can try to learn from older siblings, but more often than not takes things at his own pace and expects them to leave him alone. A single Pisces child has a great deal less personal confidence than most. He is indecisive and ruled by his emotional responses. Discipline is not easy for him, either.

As a rule, a Piscean second child may have even less confidence, but might turn to an older child for protection more than advice and/or guidance. As a second child, little Pisces quickly finds his best level and settles into a routine all his own. He does not like change for the sake of it. Nor does he appreciate anything new being forced upon him. He prefers at all times to stick with things he knows to be tried and trusted.

It is very difficult for Pisces to be the third child. Because there is so much rivalry, friendly or otherwise, between brothers and sisters, his early years may be very unsettled. The number three child has to work hard to make his mark on the world. From an early age, little Pisces does not find it easy to adapt, but can be more resourceful than people think.

In most Pisces there is a very hard streak. If he tries to rule the roost at home, he can be almost despotic. The idea of an iron fist in a velvet glove may not sound like a Pisces in the normal sense, so be warned! He will not tolerate any nonsense from anyone – and that includes his parents. If this is allowed to get out of hand, it will be very difficult indeed to bring him back to book.

In such cases, his peers will have a tough time trying to get along and be compatible with him. When he puts his mind to it, he will do his utmost to have his own way all the time, develop a selfish streak second to none and can display all the qualities of negative leadership.

At school, a Pisces child responds well to a kindly teacher who recognises his sensitivity and is prepared to try to appeal to his creativity. If the teacher takes time to draw him out, he will soon find that he has a extremely talented and artistic child on his hands.

Pisces individuals are basically introverts at any age and tend to be rather closed personalities. They are not overly adaptable and often seem quite yielding until they draw the line. They can be most perceptive and versatile, especially where people are concerned and if the mood so takes them.

15

Cusp Babies

People born on or between dates two or three days before or after the Sun changes signs are known as Cusp Babies.

There is always something special about them. They are different, and do seem to have the gift to succeed for good or ill.

This chapter will go a long way to settling the minds of parents who feel their child appears to have special gifts, but cannot quite understand why, astrologically speaking.

These dates – can and do – vary slightly from year to year because of anomalies in calculations between sidereal (astronomical) time and civil, or clock time.

Sun Sign	From	Approximately To
Aries	19 March	23 March
Taurus	18 April	22 April
Gemini	19 May	23 May
Cancer	20 June	24 June
Leo	21 July	25 July
Virgo	21 August	25 August
Libra	21 September	25 September
Scorpio	21 October	25 October
Sagittarius	20 November	24 November
Capricorn	20 December	24 December
Aquarius	18 January	22 January
Pisces	17 February	21 February

As the Sun is either in one sign or another, it cannot be in two signs at the same time, so the actual moment of change is always of some importance.

After reading the foregoing regarding their particular youngster, some parents may still have a few doubts. Perhaps something does not feel quite right because it doesn't seem to relate to their character and personality. This chapter will go a long way to supplying many of the answers.

If your offspring was born within two or possibly three days of the end of one Sun-sign, or two or three days into the beginning of a new sign, your child is a cusp baby.

Astrologers define a cusp as the imaginary line that divides the end of one house or sign and the beginning of the next house or sign. This is a very important division and has many influences in a birth chart. Look at figure 1 on page 14. On this hand-drawn birth chart, you will see at the nine o'clock position the symbol for Taurus, with the number 13 underneath it. This means that the cusp of the first house of this chart begins at the 13th degree of Taurus. Thus Taurus is the rising sign or the ascendant. To be more precise, the ascendant is 13° Taurus. In a hand-drawn chart it is customary to emphasise this point and other important features in red.

The cusp, the imaginary dividing line between Aries and Taurus, is located in the middle of the twelfth house. The cusp (or the imaginary dividing line between Taurus and Gemini) will be found in the middle of the first house. This is more clearly illustrated in the computer print-out chart on page 15. The outer circle depicts the ascendant at the nine o'clock position as 'asc.' The symbols for the signs follow in their correct sequence around the wheel.

If at the time of birth or the creation of a map of the heavens 15° Sagittarius was rising, that would be the cusp or the beginning of the first house or the ascendant of that chart. The inner circle contains the cusps of the signs along with all the planetary symbols, showing in which house and sign they are. All the subsequent cusps between the signs will also be found in the middle of each subsequent house around the chart.

For those unfamiliar with this symbology, the large panel at the bottom left of the page is to help you to interpret the symbols which are written in the shorthand of astrology.

A planet always exerts a strong influence when it is on the cusp of a house or sign, but in particular any planet located on the cusp of the ascendant will wield an exceptionally strong influence over the whole of the chart.

Angular cusps, those between houses three and four, six and seven, and nine and ten, are generally considered by most astrologers as the next most powerful and influential, but tempered largely by the sign they occupy.

However, we are more interested in the cusps of the Sun-signs. In each case we will consider these as the last two or three degrees of the end of one sign and the first two or three of the following sign. Actual calendar dates are difficult to give here because the Sun can – and does – change signs on different dates in different years, but the usually accepted dates for the Sun's entry into each sign are:

SUN SIGN	DATE OF ENTRY
Aries	21 March
Taurus	20 April
Gemini	21 May
Cancer	22 June
Leo	23 July
Virgo	23 August
Libra	23 September
Scorpio	23 October
Sagittarius	22 November
Capricorn	22 December
Aquarius	20 January
Pisces	19 February

As the Sun is either in one sign or another and cannot be in two signs at the same time, the actual moment of change has to be of importance. When the Sun transfers its energies from one sign to another, some of the first sign's characteristics must inevitably go with it. As they meet up with influences of the following sign, they either blend or fight each other for supremacy. The influence of a sign cannot – and does not – stop at the cusp.

Therefore, people born at this time must by definition have more opportunities and advantages open to them than most. Of course, the reverse of this also occurs . . . and double the problems are likely!

The individual capabilities of the person concerned now become two-fold and double-edged, tempered by the two signs involved.

Aries/Taurus

Fiery Aries is not really compatible with Earthy Taurus. However, it is still a powerful combination. Aries extrovert energies do not blend well with the rather stubborn side of Taurus. While the Aries nature is to be out and about, enthusiastically exploring and pioneering, Taurus wants to stay at home and consolidate what he already has. This child does both – and rather well.

There is a power complex here. This youngster will seize every opportunity to accumulate whatever he can and whenever he can. He sets great store by achievement and possession. He is unlikely to hold back waiting to be asked; he will be at the front selecting for himself what he thinks he can use to the best advantage. Sometimes he may be generous with his possessions and share quite happily with others. At other times, it is like getting blood out of a stone.

There will probably be some initial difficulty in learning how to relate with people, whether they are family, neighbours or total strangers. But once he decides to make friends, he will be extremely loyal and devoted, not to mention the way he thinks he should also be a bodyguard.

He is likely to have many dreams and ideals, and not be afraid to voice them. Should you criticise him, he is blunt, to the point and rather rude if you persist. He will spend a lot of time and patience trying to solve problems, but also exhibit a lazy streak second to none.

Taurus/Gemini

Earthy Taurus combines reasonably well with Airy Gemini. As these two quite separate forces combine in this short changeover period, this individual will be able to call on plenty of reserves of energy. He is impulsive, unlikely to be over-emotional and may seem insensitive to some. He makes up for this by being sociable.

Essentially, he never really grows up and always appears young at heart. He gets on well with others while still young, but as he grows never forgets how to communicate with them. He is so versatile, full of ideas and ready to learn. Mostly, he is a human dynamo, pausing just long enough to collect his breath, have a quick bite to eat and then be off again.

Make sure you protect him from inclement weather because with a sudden temperature change he becomes prone to chesty colds. He will dress – or be dressed – in the morning as the mood takes him and still be in the same clothes even if a blizzard is raging outside.

Do not be surprised if when going into his room you find another child or children in there. They will be doing his bidding while he is off elsewhere making the whole plan come together. He loves to be in the middle of whatever is happening at all times, but does not take too kindly to discipline. The severest way to deal with him is to keep him in, curtailing his activities. And the excuses he makes in his defence must be heard to be believed. This is one garrulous child at the best of times.

Gemini/Cancer

Airy Gemini and Watery Cancer are not entirely unsympathetic to each other. Often, a youngster with a combination of these two elements will produce an extremely positive personality. The outgoing nature of Gemini can sometimes conflict badly with the usually stay-at-home Cancerian. Both signs can cause changeable personalities. Nowhere is this better emphasised than here.

This child is liable to be a never-ending source of surprise to his parents and all his contemporaries, many of whom may not sustain the effort of coping with his many moods, so could just drift away. Such a child tends to have very few real friends, but a whole host of acquaintances from all walks. He is extremely affectionate, highly sensitive and feels things very deeply. In league with a Geminian urge to communicate, this often leads to creative pursuits, such as teaching, writing or similar forms of creativity.

Because Cancerians love their domestic environment so much, they could well develop an interest, later a hobby, then an occupation that can be enjoyed from home. The present developing computer world is ideal for his mentality. Surfing the net must be an attraction that few of this changeover period would choose to ignore.

Relationships are often made with people more outgoing than he is. Cancerians and Geminians are both fairly selfish, though in slightly different ways. Cancer is emotional, Gemini is intellectual, but both need to be with others. Both are devoted to causes. Together in one character, it makes for an interesting and complex personality.

Cancer/Leo

The Watery, emotional sign of Cancer is far from compatible with the Fiery, active sign of Leo. Emotionally volatile, never still for long, these youngsters must learn to control their feelings as early as possible, not just for their own sake, but for those around them as well. There is an acute need for self-control at all times. The sooner this is established, the better.

Once this has been realised, these folk can get on with their lives. In business, sport or almost any other activity they are likely to be extremely successful. Many reach the top while still young and stay there, provided, of course, they have some kind of inner personal stability.

They like to take risks, aim high and love change in almost all aspects of their lives. The challenge of a dare, irrespective of any inherent danger, can be a drug to some.

These youngsters enjoy travel for almost any reason – visiting friends or new places of interest, for business or just simply for the pleasure of being on the move. Moving house attracts them, so many are likely to change their address several times despite all the hassle that goes with it.

For some, this is not exactly realistic, but then these people are not always realists. They create their own world. Should their friends not like it, that's tough! Incredibly ambitious, always ready to pursue their dreams at the drop of a hat, they set the pace and never stop. Boring easily, when low, they are extremely depressed. Self-discipline is essential to them.

Leo/Virgo

The Fiery, active nature of Leo can blend well with the Earthy, practical Virgo characteristics. The tendency here is for this type to have one of two natures. They will either seem full of life, constantly on the move, friendly and open or quite the reverse: difficult to know or understand, secretive, subtle and rather careful.

This youngster learns how to handle power very early, for good or ill, but is always trustworthy. Others know they can use him as a sounding board for their own ideas and plans, give information freely and allow him access to all manner of secrets. In return, he maintains their trust by keeping his own counsel. This cusp baby always has a quiet air of competence and authority throughout life. In childhood, contemporaries choose not to take him on probably because they are unsure of the outcome. When older, he is a natural for positions of responsibility.

These young folk tend not to share their innermost thoughts and dreams with anyone, but if they do, or when they decide on their future partner, they often choose just the right person. As a parent, if you oppose their choice, you risk losing them so do be very careful in this area.

Such characters may seem cold or unfeeling, but this is far from the truth. They do not like showing their emotions, except when becoming frustrated by red tape. Strangely, they often make good petty bureaucrats themselves.

Virgo/Libra

Earthy Virgo and Airy Libra usually blend well together and often produce personalities to do with the artistic or creative worlds. Born idealists, they make every effort always to appear as neat and tidy as possible. In later life, personal appearance and all that is associated with dress and deportment are important.

These types can be obsessive. They develop an idea or hatch a plan and pursue it to the bitter end. They often become experts in jewellery, clothes, personal hygiene or the health and fitness fields. Emotionally, there may be quite a few problems, especially during adolescence. In purely practical terms, the Virgo side of their nature is not all that outgoing. The Libran half of their character always has to be with people if they are to function properly. As this type is often quite attractive physically, they have to learn not only to cope with this, but must also be prepared for the attitude of their parents. Their mums and dads have to walk the tightrope. It is one thing to be pushy, but if you overdo it, you can easily create unnecessary problems for your youngster.

Travel always appeals to this group, especially if it has anything to with furthering knowledge in a practical sense. They like to learn, and are likely to store all manner of little bits and pieces of information for later use. They make good mediators for they know how to listen and then pin-point the nub of a problem. This is a natural gift as they are adept at making good judgements in such situations.

Libra/Scorpio

The Airy, Cardinal and intellectual nature of Libra does not sit too well with the Watery, Fixed and emotional Scorpio at the best of times. Libra likes company as does Scorpio, but for different reasons. Libra enjoys the free, happy-go-lucky atmosphere of a general relationship. Scorpio requires a much more personal and deeper association, preferably on a one-to-one basis.

Either way, this group needs some understanding because of the moods they suffer. That is the right word – because others also have to suffer with them! However, one good thing about them is their innate ability to judge people at a first meeting. If they allow their natural sixth sense to operate properly, they rarely fall foul of anyone.

Their rather fixed nature makes them as many enemies as friends. There are rarely any half-measures because of their difficult mood swings.

From an early age, these youngsters have a sharp mind and a cutting wit. They are perceptive and quite fearless having chosen their path. If you are foolish enough to ask one for an honest appraisal you will get it . . . straight from the shoulder.

This group often works behind the scenes in occupations that carry an air of mystery – medical, police or other similar types of investigatory tasks. They are equally at home on the stage in front of everyone in the diverse field of entertainment. In many cases this hazardous profession may be the only one to match their intense personalities.

Scorpio/Sagittarius

The Fixed and slightly reserved nature of Scorpio combines easily with the Fiery and freedom-loving Sagittarius personality. Here, perhaps more than anywhere else in this study of cusp babies do we find an in-built rebel streak second to none. If the stubborn Scorpio nature makes any inroads, this youngster will take some handling.

Curiously, despite the rebelliousness and a constant avoidance of responsibility, this soul means no harm to anyone and would be horrified if he was accused of doing so. He is a natural wild-child who has to do his own thing. Discipline can be just a word unless you come down early and heavily. You must show who is boss and make them respect rules and regulations.

Pure Sagittarians often become pillars of society during or after middle age, and this group are no exception. Eventually, they seem to grow up and mature.

In essence, they matured much earlier, but just did not want to be identified with the Establishment. Socially, they are born to lead and will always be found in a group somewhere. When it comes to industry, few are their equal. Intellectually, they can outsmart the best. It is often the way with those who prefer to break the rules for then they can happily re-write them and feel no remorse when they break them as well. They are naturally intuitive, and have no fear of authority. What they really want is a better society, so try their best to make something of the environment for everyone.

Sagittarius/Capricorn

This rich mixture of opposites provides one of the most serious and responsible personalities of all the cusp babies. At a very early age this youngster will adopt a serious attitude to almost everything he does at play or work. He probably chooses a career equally as early, striving to be the best in his field at all times.

This group does not suffer fools. Nor will they help people who show no semblance of helping themselves. They often seem quiet and unassuming and, in many cases, unapproachable. However, this is far from the truth. They are natural leaders and not only want positions of authority, but expect them, so much so that at interviews their confidence helps them win through.

They are not very good at expressing their inner feelings except to a few tried and trusted friends. They feel things very deeply, and do not like to make, or be seen to make, mistakes.

When they get an idea, this group will research and sound out people who matter and value the feedback. Once they start something, it will be finished – properly! Because of their success at getting things done, they tend to accumulate money and possessions early. They also enjoy travel, for it gives them a chance to relax and also learn.

If they have a lesson to learn, it is to lighten up, to be much more at ease socially. They must be less self-critical. This is a Fire and Earth mixture: the lack of the lightness of an Air sign and the sensitivity of a Water sign shows.

Capricorn/Aquarius

Here, two quite opposed types constantly vie for supremacy which, as a rule, makes for a quite unforgettable character. The serious Capricorn, with both feet always firmly on the ground, must blend with the Airy and Fixed Aquarian ideals.

If ever there was a group which makes its presence felt, it is this one. They have a razor-sharp wit and perception to match. Never really sure of what they may do next, they are always full of fun and vitality. It is frequently said that you cannot keep a good Geminian down: this group is in much the same vein.

Their forte is creative energy. When constructive Capricorn gives way to allow ambitious Aquarius full rein to his ideas, the result is often of benefit for all. Overflowing with innovation, most young-sters in this group can easily be accused of being born before their time. They have an innate cleverness that gets to the nitty-gritty of a problem long before anyone else.

However, they are also liable to get carried away in a fantasy world and not appreciate the more practical and mundane side of life which we must all observe. This youngster has to be raised in a stable domestic situation with parents prepared to give more of their time than usual to establish a solid foundation from which the child may always work.

These children have rather wild mood swings brought about by not understanding why they cannot pursue their dreams because normal duties and obligations have to be attended to first. The stress and tension this creates needs constructive relief.

Aquarius/Pisces

This youngster is highly sensitive, a great humanitarian and one who feels things very deeply. Acutely aware of all that is going on, it is difficult for them to become settled. While Airy Aquarius mixes well with the sensitivity of Watery Pisces, it serves to create an unusual character. However, there is little or no stability to offset all the airy-fairyness of everything.

These children are likely to be visionaries all their lives. They may be seen to live in a permanent world of their own making, but could well develop prescience and become involved in mysticism and allied fields. They love freedom and prefer to exist the way they decide. If at work, they do their best, and some excel in the business world.

Many are career-minded, but it can take time before deciding in which direction they ought to go. While the arts attract, they should be talked away from the performing arts. Their nature is not suited for the criticism that can be levelled in this area. They tend to work better in composing, painting or writing, perhaps prose or verse. In short, anything in the background. For those who need to prove themselves, this is a much better arena in which to develop their creativity.

The more mundane side of life can be a struggle for many born in this period for the harsh realities of everyday existence are not really their forte unless they have a partner willing to take on all the responsibility, theirs included. But never underestimate them: many have a steel backbone . . . as would-be critics have found to their cost!

Pisces/Aries

All the sensitivity and idealism of Pisces combines positively with Aries emotional and physical drive. The tendency is to be open, outspoken and frank. This child is very passionate and direct. Generally speaking, what he wants, he gets.

This group does not take too kindly to opposition of any kind, merited or otherwise, so anyone who tries to interfere generally regrets it. He is often misunderstood because of his directness. He can move very swiftly to achieve an aim, but it is this speed that tends to defeat the competition: they simply do not expect it.

This youngster seems to know his own mind at an early age and goes all out for what he wants once he has made a decision. If he realises he is not going to succeed by conventional means, he will bluff with the best of them. His aims can be unrealistic at times. Coupled with his impatience, it is not surprising that he makes enemies.

Those in this group have natural leadership abilities. They recognise that others must be encouraged, and give credit where it is due. But they are also practical and will dismiss anyone who does not pull their weight. Friendships are easily won and lost on such a basis.

Friends are very unwise to criticise without just cause for these youngsters are incredibly sensitive to criticism of any kind, but are not averse to dishing it out themselves. Where others sit back and are not willing to take a chance and risk the odds, those from this group will have a go. You cannot ask for more than that from anyone, adult or child.

To sum up, these dual-natured types are very different from the run-of-the-mill basic Sun-sign people. While still very young, they need all the help they can get from adults who recognise the signs and take time to be as supportive as they can.

Provided this guidance is positive, when these little ones grow into adulthood the dominant influence within is liable to be much easier for them to contend with.

16

Chinese Astrology Children

The Chinese Calendar, 1985–2005

The Chinese lunar calendar is the longest in the world and began in 2637 BC. The full sequence lasts 60 years and is subdivided into five minor cycles of 12 years each. It is not a fixed cycle because it is a lunar calendar, based on the Moon's motion. Our western calendar is based on the Sun's motion and is constant.

The Chinese New Year always starts at the time of the second New Moon after the Winter Solstice of the previous year.

In Chinese astrology, the whole year is considered to be most fortunate. Thus, if you are a Tiger, the whole of that year is a highly propitious period. It is rather like having your birthday all year round instead of just one day!

Year	Duration		Animal
1985	20 February 1985	08 February 1986	Ox
1986	09 February 1986	28 January 1987	Tiger
1987	29 January 1987	16 February 1988	Rabbit
1988	17 February 1988	05 February 1989	Dragon
1989	06 February 1989	26 January 1990	Snake
1990	27 January 1990	14 February 1991	Horse
1991	15 February 1991	03 February 1992	Sheep
1992	04 February 1992	22 January 1993	Monkey
1993	23 January 1993	09 February 1994	Rooster
1994	10 February 1994	30 January 1995	Dog
1995	31 January 1995	18 February 1996	Pig
1996	19 February 1996	07 February 1997	Rat
1997	08 February 1997	27 January 1998	Ox
1998	28 January 1998	15 February 1999	Tiger
1999	16 February 1999	04 February 2000	Rabbit

2000	05 February 2000	23 January 2001	Dragon
2001	24 January 2001	11 February 2002	Snake
2002	12 February 2002	31 January 2003	Horse
2003	01 February 2003	21 January 2004	Sheep
2004	22 January 2004	08 February 2005	Monkey
2005	09 February 2005	28 January 2006	Rooster

The Young Rat

Young Rats, like their adult counterparts, tend to fall into two camps. One can appear to be sweet and loving, full of charm, sensitive to a fault, clever and responsible. The other will seem to be cold, calculating, jealous, possessive and selfish.

In essence, all Rats have these characteristics in the one personality. They are adept at hiding their real, inner feelings, but if disturbed by injustice or unfairness, any of these traits will be employed to restore the status quo.

A Rat youngster starts to demonstrate a calculating nature rather early. He has to have the larger part if something is divided into two, or the odd one over, if there is one.

He never misses a trick. He always knows where his things are, even how or where he left them. Don't try to take away what you think is an old toy assuming he won't miss it. He does not like to part with anything, but neither he is a hoarder.

He may mother or nurse other youngsters or boss and bully them. At his best, he is a good friend, at worst an enemy to respect.

Young Rats are avid readers. They like to learn and appreciate the written word because of the many different experiences a good read can bring. He will express himself well because he absorbs so quickly. Because many Rats enjoy the art of expression they are often well-known for it in later years.

He usually gets on well with nearly everybody, but could exhibit a slight air of reserve, just enough to make you think before you take him for anything. Normally, he has a charming social sense, knows how to put others at their ease and is the life and soul of a party. At the same time, he will also use the opportunity – especially if it is his party – to meet people specially invited so he can persuade them to his way of thinking for other purposes. After all, Rats do not like to waste anything . . . and that includes their time!

The Young Ox

One thing is for sure: this is no cry-baby. He is tough, rugged and quite a stubborn and determined character. If necessary, he will turn the world upside down to put things right, in his eyes.

He loves and treasures his personal privacy, but is not over fussy about much else. The few concessions he does ask for may be made more in the way of a demand than a request.

The young Ox takes well to discipline. In fact, he can be almost regimental at times. He will take on board any schedule made for him and may insist on having meals at the same time each day, but won't be over-demanding about their content. Like any other child, he has his likes and dislikes, and you learn early enough about them. There is a place for everything, and everything has its place. He has a penchant for regularity, of knowing where everything is and what is expected of him. He is always neat and tidy in all that he does, either at home or away from his usual environment.

A young Ox can assume the mantle of responsibility if you let him take charge when you are going to be away. This is the best child a teacher could choose when they have leave the classroom for a short time.

He is not overly influenced or taken in by smooth talk. If he has to be won over, make it a definite instruction. Mostly, his is an unbiased view of life, so if he is to have your respect and not argue about details or anything else pertinent to the exercise at hand, you must treat him almost as you would an adult.

This character does not readily show his feelings because he is basically a very private person, easily hurt by a wrong word or deed, which few suspect. He is naive emotionally, may not always understand the harsh realities of life or be able to show his emotions and express his sense of humour.

However, because he can be so reliable he soon gains the respect of those around him. The young Ox often becomes a good leader in later life.

The Young Tiger

These youngsters grow up as happy and cheerful mini-adults who can be great fun or demented terrorists at one and the same time.

The young tiger is irrepressible, full of life, active and always to be found in the thick of everything. He throws himself into whatever is going on. Even if you try to keep something quiet, he has the knack of finding out and joining in. Difficult to hold back or rein in, he seems to be able to present a bright and confident face to the world, so much so that few really know what he is thinking. He can talk the hind leg from a donkey, and bluff and counter-bluff so well that even his parents cannot be really sure of him.

He has an insatiable curiosity. If the mood so takes him, he will spend hours following up whatever it is that has caught his attention, often to the exclusion of all else. When in this mood, he may not always see the pitfalls, if any, and can get caught up in all sorts of predicaments. He is known to bully others into his way of thinking. Those less aggressive or unable to think on their feet in like manner become natural targets for his enthusiasm, but no ill is intended.

Despite this rather forceful attitude, he has an equally natural gift for making and keeping friends. People are drawn to him by his warm and affectionate personality. He expresses feelings openly and directly. The young Tiger has strong opinions and doesn't hold back when airing his views. He does not trust lightly or easily. But once he makes friends and learns to how to trust, the relationship could be life-long.

He needs a good, strong discipline at a very early age because if he is allowed to go unchecked for too long he can easily tip the scales and become uncontrollable. The sooner he is made to know this, the better for all concerned. While not always a smooth childhood, it will fun. Having him around is a reward in itself.

The Young Rabbit
A junior Rabbit is a highly sensitive and very emotional child. He will exhibit mood swings that can defy gravity at times or just sit quietly on his own and play for hours with one or two toys.

When not throwing a moody, he is fairly even-tempered, polite and most obedient. His manners can be impeccable. Even if he does climb onto his high horse, he is rarely deliberately offensive, but can be very cutting with certain remarks. The trouble here is that while he is being hurtful, his observations are also truthful. He is very perceptive, especially where people are concerned, often seeing both sides of a question far earlier than most. When arguing, junior Rabbit does so intelligently.

Perhaps more than any other sign, it is essential for the young Rabbit to have a stable background and the warmth of a good home, plenty of love and attention, and guidance from an early age.

At times, it will be hard to know what he is thinking or why he has acted the way he has. Adept at hiding his feelings when he wants to, he will say or do things he knows will please you. As a diplomat, he can excel; as a mediator, he wins hands down. This youngster is more than able to fend for himself, extremely protective of what is his and works his chances out so well that he does not often get caught.

Junior Rabbit doesn't flout the rules, but rewrites them to suit his particular situation. The magic word here is subtle so when you are going to meet a Rabbit to sort out a problem, you might just as well give up and let him have his own way because if you do not, he will take it anyway.

He learns to adopt a rather philosophical outlook early in life, outwardly shrugs off set-backs easily, then starts all over again. The Rabbit tends to have few really close friends, but a wide circle of acquaintances from all walks, and is usually held in high esteem by adults and contemporaries alike.

The Young Dragon
This child is very intense and often carries this trait through to adulthood. He is an idealist par excellence, well able to look after himself and usually becomes quite independent at a very age.

The young Dragon tends to look at everything with a different eye to most people. He has the ability to adapt to his circumstances, but because he really does not like to ask for help unless absolutely necessary, will change and innovate what he wants, when he wants and how he wants it.

Basically, he is a good child. Rarely outwardly disrespectful or wilful, sometimes he questions the reasons why certain actions or decisions were taken if unable to understand them. Whilst an out-and-out idealist from a very young age, he is also quite practical.

Most young Dragons are avid readers. He needs to feed his vivid imagination constantly. In this area, parents must keep a watchful eye to ensure this does not get out of hand because if carried to extremes, there will be no holding him.

He might become a bully or be bullied because of his beliefs and ideals. Although bright and fairly independent, he can also develop hero worship, the object of his thoughts being a teacher at the least or a film actor at the worst, someone he considers worthy of his affections. He is often very ambitious and not afraid to voice opinions in a desire to achieve his aims. There is rarely anything personal in any of his disagreements with others. He just needs to feel that he making his contribution to the matter at hand, whatever it is. He always means well, is sincere and responds to praise.

When the young Dragon falls short of your expectations at any time, you must spend time to explain the facts of the matter, reassure him, show him where he went wrong and he will soon bounce back.

Dragons like to feel they will not disappoint those who have faith in them. They really are a joy to have around.

The Young Snake

As both a child and an adult, a Snake gets along in his own way with most, but when someone upsets him he becomes spiteful and an unrelenting enemy. He will sulk, be vindictive and most temperamental until he gets his way or pays back the crime against him.

In many ways, young Snakes are complex characters, quiet and very observant. His intelligence should never be questioned. He will demonstrate just how clever exactly at the right time, either by a confident statement or a determined action. He makes up his mind about what he really wants fairly early on in life, then shows how practical he is by achieving that aim under his own steam. He does not do things by halves for he is a realist.

Most young Snakes tend to be independent, studious and prepared to work hard at school. He responds a little too readily if you want to spoil him for some reason. When you do, make sure it is only a treat or he might expect it all the time.

By nature, young Snakes are solitary, secretive and brooding. He is not averse to social matters, but it will probably be on his terms when he does join in. He keeps himself to himself, not taking kindly to those who try to get too close. However, when he does make friends, they last and last.

He is capable of leadership at an early age. Just how he manages to get himself into positions of influence may remain a mystery – and in some cases it might be better if it did! He is fair, but it is his lust for power that people might question. It is probably to demonstrate his talents and abilities on his terms, but can leave him open to criticism. Once again, it may not show on the surface because he is good at hiding his feelings in such matters.

Then again, most young Snakes become successful when they grow up. And you cannot argue with that!

The Young Horse

Generally speaking, little Horses are likeable, popular and full of energy. They love life, and are always doing something. Rarely still for long, they have mercurial minds. Many Horses grow up into careers or vocations where they have to be clever with their hands.

The little Horse relishes outdoor pursuits, and is always willing to take part in all manner of physical exercises and adventures. However, at the end of the day he will turn up at home ravenous, ready for an eight-course meal! He tends to balance a rather positive and enthusiastic approach to life with a stubborn, wilful and disobedient nature. In fairness, when he is held to task for any wrong-doing, he accepts the blame and will not snitch on his co-conspirators.

The young Horse resents restriction. When unwell and cooped up in his room, he has to be told in no uncertain terms why he he must stay there or is straight out the window or back door.

Life is a challenge for these impulsive rascals. He does not respond too well to discipline. Although a realist in so many other ways, he has a nasty temper and does not always seem to learn by experiences. But sooner or later he will meet up with someone better than he is at such things, then becomes a more positive little chap with whom to deal.

It is only after he realises how far he can push his luck that he begins to develop a particular charm. He learns how to worm his way into your good books. The young Horse seeks out your weaknesses and plays on them until he gets what he wants. There are many folk who still wonder how Horses manage to get the better of them.

Constantly full of ideas, with many irons in many fires and stretching himself too thin at times, he is likely to shelve a project only on a temporary basis. But he is always ready to breathe new life into an old idea at any time, so beware.

The Young Sheep

The young Sheep is mild-mannered, creative and essentially a blessing to his parents. He is in his element when being fussed over or spoiled. He is rather dependent, emotional, and always vulnerable.

Sensitive, kind and generous, he makes as many friends as enemies because he is such a gentle soul. A perfect target for bullies, he may have a difficult later childhood and, of course, might cause a few attendance problems.

Few Sheep become leaders. Much better as one of the flock, they are happiest in the middle of a friendly crowd. Little Sheep look to those more dominant in their circle and allow themselves to become part of that society.

Many little Sheep are blessed with a vividly fertile imagination, easily influenced or adversely affected if feeling low. When rejected, they withdraw into a world of their own making – and it could prove to be very difficult to draw them out.

The Sheep is a home-lover. He does not like to stray too far and tends to stay on long after other children have flown the nest. However, when he decides to fend for himself and set up home you will recognise it the moment you enter. He is a traditionalist with an in-built sense of taste. He likes old-fashioned ideas, but combines them with every modern labour-saving device you can imagine. The Sheep wants his home to be a home, not just a house. He loves food, but has a sensible approach to diet and keep fit regimes. Both the boys and girls of this sign are domesticated and make excellent cooks.

He makes the best of friends, being compassionate, generous and ever loyal. He is extremely affectionate and will identify with your problems. A born diplomat, he can keep secrets and be trusted with anything and everything. In return, he asks the same of you, but is often disappointed unless, of course, you happen to be another Sheep.

The Young Monkey

If ever there were a real imp of the oriental zodiac, the Monkey child is it. Bright-eyed and bushy-tailed, sociable, gregarious and so predictably unpredictable, he is everything to all people at all times.

Changeable, bubbly and witty, the Monkey youngster knows just how to communicate at all levels and ages. He understands people and their weaknesses, knows what makes them tick and exploits every trick in the book to get what he wants from them.

He is not still for very long for it just isn't in his nature. When very young, you will soon discover he has a low boredom threshold. It is always wise to know where he is and what he is supposed to be doing because if it has all gone quiet he might be dissecting his father's electric razor or re-wiring your hair-dryer. The young Monkey has a taste for taking anything electrical or mechanical apart because such gadgetry fascinates him.

An inner drive compels him to improve all the time. There is a gift for accumulating knowledge, and he is able to concentrate on several things at once. He absorbs a lot of knowledge on his travels and can always be relied upon to supply information on anything just when it is needed the most.

The young Monkey has no scruples when something goes wrong. He will bend or break the rules to escape retribution as such things are for mortals, not Monkeys. His optimism keeps him ever hopeful. It is not in his nature to admit defeat: he just tries and tries again until he does succeed.

While he can be selfish and puts himself first most of the time, he is careful with those less fortunate and may be discovered in the background quietly working to help them. He will not make a song and dance of it, but simply shrug it off.

The Monkey child has many friends from all walks because he attracts people like a magnet with his freedom-loving ways. You are likely to find him in the middle of anything, at any time with anybody who will put up with him and his antics!

The Young Rooster

A born self-starter, the young Rooster spends a lot of time probing for more information about anything that catches his eye at the time. He is a good pupil and learns quickly.

Generally, he is neat and tidy and can be quite methodical. If allowed to get out of hand, this makes him impossible to live with. He takes well to discipline, and can be difficult to deal with if permitted to instigate a programme involving his contemporaries.

Usually, children do not take kindly to being ordered about by one of their own. He has a critical eye and tongue and will not hesitate to let you know what he thinks. Our young Rooster is not rude, just straightforward, and in many cases can be a joy to have around if things look like going wrong. For some adults, especially the parents of other children, this is not entirely acceptable. While he may not care too much, they might. He speaks his mind as he sees fit, but after a while soon endears himself to them.

Young Roosters are born optimists and tend to pursue their plans with a blithe abandon. It is very rare for them to change horses mid-stream so they may not always listen to advice once they have made up their mind. On the negative side, they are often blind to their own faults. It is rare for them to be wrong – in their eyes!

Perhaps this attitude is brought about because the young Rooster is also extremely competitive and adventurous, apt to try anything once, twice if he likes it. He will put his talents to almost anything if he feels it can prove to be profitable. Thus, when he is up, he is on top of the world with rather too many 'friends' always willing to share in his profits.

But when he is down, there are very few folk around to help him pick up the pieces. However, he has a natural resilience that copes well with such times. It does not take him long to bounce back.

The Young Dog

Most young Dogs are happy little souls unless someone does the wrong thing at the wrong time for the wrong reasons. Then this child will demonstrate clearly and precisely why you will never, ever do so again. Eventually, he might forget the incident. But he may not always forgive.

Usually, he is cheerful, though perhaps a shade too forthright for a child. His natural sense of justice will not allow a slight or an unfair practice to go uncorrected. A young Dog won't permit anyone to bully him or his friends: he will oppose it in such a way that it does not happen again, certainly not with the same adversary.

He is nearly always confident, consistent and reasonably sensible. He will deal with his school work or other duties in more than a satisfactory manner, and is reasonable if is asked to help around the house.

The young Dog tends to adopt an independent air which, in some cases, could easily be misconstrued as a rebel streak. But he rarely oversteps the mark. He is known and liked for his rather candid sense of humour and generally warm nature.

However, if upset, he will rebel. While his anger flares up pretty quickly, it can be all over in a few moments and everything returns to normal.

If he feels his parents do not appreciate him for any reason, the young Dog might become insensitive or difficult to handle. Just a simple 'Please' or 'Thank you' work wonders here and he becomes much more co-operative. Basically, he is co-operative so this might not occur, but if it should, try not to threaten him to get what you desire. Simply take the time to explain what you want, let him see the error of his ways and he will be like putty in your hands.

Despite all the foregoing, he rarely exhibits prejudice, and avoids unpleasantness. You can trust him with anything. Give him the chance and he will surprise you at how good he can be. He sets a high standard early in life, and it nearly always shows.

The Young Pig

A little Pig is reasonably self-reliant, sociable and fairly easy to get along with provided he is given a certain amount of leeway to express himself properly. He is a rather determined character, one who likes to take the lead in school activities. He is resilient, so set-backs will be taken in his stride. This youngster can demonstrate personal courage when he has to, for is not one to complain. Injuries on the sports field are a matter of fact. In this event, he can stand a good deal of pain.

Young Pigs have a healthy appetite: you won't have to worry too much or pamper him in this area! He works and plays hard. On balance, he tends to use his energies well. You might not always know what he is thinking because he can put on a poker face to mask his true feelings. He may not need too much attention emotionally, but must feel he has your support when or if things go wrong.

Something of an individualist, this character often projects a give-and-take attitude, which makes him popular with his contemporaries and others with whom he comes into contact. He has good organising ability, knowing how to calm people down and smooth things over. It is not really his nature to take sides, but if he does he makes an excellent friend and ally.

The young Pig can take positive criticism because he puts all his strengths and convictions into various undertakings. With his softly, softly approach and gentle persuasiveness, he can entice most people to help him out one way or another.

Should you do him a favour, he will pay you back three-fold . . . for good or ill! If he has any serious drawbacks, it is that he can be totally blind to the faults of those he loves, for his loyalty to friends is unquestioned. He has an instinctive understanding of another person's emotions, but not always of his own. He usually has a great zest for living.

17

Parents and Children

Obviously, we were all children once. Now that many of us are parents, it might not hurt to have an astrological look at ourselves as such. We have learned how to understand our youngsters a little better by using basic astrological techniques. If it works in one direction, it must also do so the other way. What sort of parents do people of the various signs make? Let's find out!

Aries

Both parents are inclined to act independently of each other, which does not help the child caught between the two of you. If you are in your usual impulsive mood, your tolerance levels can become strained, to say the least. In some cases, this is likely to rub off on the child.

You do not mean to be like it, but you are an Aries. Your time is not only precious to you, but is to your children as well. You both care for them, so make the quality time to be with them as individuals. Give your undivided attention when you are with them, and make it a regular event.

Aries Mother

You relish the challenges of being a mother, but can be a little sharp-tongued if your children ask too many questions or get in the way of what you want to do, when you want to do it because of your built-in Aries selfish streak. Always show them affection, no matter how you feel. Curb your impulsiveness. Slow down. Aim to make your youngster feel important to you.

Aries Father

Most Aries men make good fathers, but not in the early days. You aren't used to being around anything quite so small and dependent, and tend to be so macho and independent. You have to make time to learn how to care, feed, change nappies and do all the tasks so alien to your nature. Try not to be too pushy as your youngster develops.

Taurus

Both parents are happy in the domestic environment, enjoying all the trappings of marriage and bringing up children. You often fall straight into the routine of rearing offspring as if it were a second nature. You can be rather stern disciplinarians and are not very flexible in this area.

You tend to be traditionalists and feel there is only one way to bring up a child – as your parents did, plus your own ideas. Learn to ease off a little and allow your young much more freedom of expression. You can also be somewhat stuck-in-the-mud because of your stubborn streak.

Taurus Mother

You understand how to provide a good home, are affectionate and very practical. You have the patience of a saint and appreciate when to issue short, sharp words of admonition in just the right tone for the best effect. You instinctively know what to do. Your children detect this and come to you with their problems knowing they will get a fair hearing.

Taurus Father

The ever practical do-it-yourself, down-to-earth and stable man of the house. Always there, not just for your children, but also those of others. A neighbour's youngster will ask you to mend his bike or show him how and you do so quite willingly.

As your child grows older, you may become intolerant of how he or she behaves and carries on. Remember your own youth!

Gemini

As parents, you are fairly easy-going. When you try to get youngsters to toe the line they respond well because you have a way of communication. You learned early, remembered and have never forgotten your own childhood.

Your house will nearly always be full of children, yours and the neighbours. You have ever-open doors because yours is a friendly home. You are not over-protective, but do insist on certain rules. If not observed, you can be very impatient and irritable. Children regard you more as a friend than an adult. You may be a little too pushy where your own are concerned.

Gemini Mother

Quite how you learn to be a mother can be something of a mystery because you do not seem to follow the traditional guide-lines. It is almost as if you make it up as you go along, which is probably true. However, in your need to be more of a friend than a mum you might forget discipline, your weakest point. You really are a modern mother – and your offspring love you for it!

Gemini Father

Gadget-mad and over-indulgent at times, all you really want for your children is the best. But to be so, they need to learn.

You will exert all your influence to make sure they can read and write early. You play with them and exercise their imaginations to make them use their minds. While you may not show too much physical affection, they still know you love them.

Cancer

As parents, you are in your element. The home for you is the the centre of your world. You tend to be a touch over-protective, but the need to ensure that everything is well at all times can be too strong for some. Friends who criticise may be right, but you will strongly defend your traditional ways and ideas against all-comers.

Cancerians are both mother and father to their little one. Although they have the best of intentions, they need to relax more and allow their children to experience a few knocks here and there.

Despite all this, you make your offspring feel important. They learn the proper values of life early in this house.

Cancer Mother

Simply the best of the zodiac. You show affection and encourage them openly right from the start. You identify with their crises and triumphs with equal facility, but have to learn when to let things go and not allow your imagination run riot too much if or when they are out and about. You have a long memory – and children are not allowed to forget it!

Cancer Father

You make the best provider for your family which, in your eyes, is complete only when children arrive. You will have saved for this, built that or made plans long before others think about any such matters. You either impose a harsh disciplinary regime right from the start or are lax and indifferent until it is too late – and can end up regretting it either way.

Leo

Leo parents are prone to teach more than being a mother or father to their children. Rather heavy-handed at times, you mean well, but have a knack of being too controlling. You are such natural leaders and get very disappointed when your children cannot or will not follow.

Neither of you like to take second place to anyone or anything. Your little bundle of joy is somewhat demanding, more than you are used to in the early days. Sometimes your children suffer because of unintentional forgetful moments. But as a Leo and parent you are always fun to have around.

Leo Mother

This mother is very protective and equally strict. You lay the ground rules early and expect them to be followed implicitly. You encourage your children, always making time to guide them through sticky patches so they learn through experience. This is probably because you had to at their age and have never forgotten. You also teach them independence.

Leo Father

Rather too demanding of your children, you clash with anyone who is critical of you. You know best . . . and that is the end of it!

You do not enjoy caring and nurturing for the new baby, but really are an old softie deep down. When you warm to the idea, your generosity knows no bounds. You will do your utmost to ensure the best of everything is theirs at all times.

Virgo

Virgo parents are extremely efficient, with everything organised and so under control. You are practical, having an answer for just about anything that could go wrong. You are also extremely over-protective and try to shield your youngsters from the great big world outside.

You often make the mistake of wanting for your offspring things you could not have when you were a child. Some of your ambitions for junior might really be those you never managed yourself.

You worry a lot. This can spread to your children. Encourage them by all means, but try not to be too critical. We all make mistakes. Learn to work with them, not against them.

Virgo Mother

You need to show more affection because you are not naturally a physically demonstrative type. But do not forget that cuddles mean a lot to children.

You look after all their interests perfectly, too much in many cases because you are so well organised. To you, details are a second nature. Just occasionally, make a mistake and try to look vulnerable. Your children will love you for it.

Virgo Father

You cannot have your cake and eat it. You must have a well-run home. Anyone who disturbs your routine is for the high jump.

You are not too good with children, almost afraid of them at times and far too strict! If you could climb off your high horse and down to their level, you will see what fatherhood is all about. If you want the best, let them show you.

Libra

You are born idealists in so many ways. You will limit your family to three – two to fight, and one to stop them. Neither of you like to get your hands dirty so in the beginning it can be interesting to see who changes the nappies.

You and your partner need peace and quiet. You should address this problem early. Plan out responsibilities and duties, but stay flexible. As long as you both have some time away from home and on your own, your children will profit. And in spite of all this, they will learn good manners, be graceful and be an absolute credit to you.

Libra Mother

Unfairness and injustice make your blood boil. You instil a love of fair play right from the word go. You will teach your child to appreciate the good things of life. You will also see they are raised in a stress-free domestic environment and that they have the freedom to do what they want, when they want to do it – provided it is legal!

Libra Father

You tend to appreciate parenthood more than your Libran wife in many ways, but will have to spend many hours with him or her, especially in the very early days. This will take some doing!

Discipline may be a problem, but Libra is not the diplomat of the zodiac for nothing. By the time your child becomes a young adult, you will have both learned a great deal.

Scorpio

Scorpio parents are protective and rather set in their ways so it does not pay to upset you. You lean heavily on your children in the early days to make sure they really appreciate that you are the boss! If they fail to do so, they never forget the penalty. You both tend to appear consistent, unyielding and apparently uncaring.

It is almost as if you are unprepared to treat your child as an individual. The quicker you realise that all young children are very different, the sooner you make friends with them and grow up together. Let them see your human side because you feel things so deeply – and so do other people, young or old.

Scorpio Mother

Scorpio mums can be demanding, possessive and are very well-known for their views on discipline. Strong-minded, eager for the child to learn quickly, you are the calm focal point in the family, and excel in emergencies. Your offspring soon learn to look at their problems from all aspects before taking action, a favourite trait you frequently exhibit.

Scorpio Father
A practical man, you approach parenthood as a duty to be performed well. But you are also acutely aware of your emotions and what it was like for you when you were young. You identify easily with very young children, but tend to seem a little more aloof as they grow up. But you are approachable. Not only do they know this, they trade on it!

Sagittarius
Even after you become parents, Sagittarians are still having fun growing up. You are eternally young – and never forget it.

As a result, you make good friends with your children, but they grow up basking more in the friendship than the parent and child arena. The biggest trouble is maintaining discipline.

You both enjoy freedom of expression, but can suffer from quick changes of mood. What you ignore at lunch time becomes a heinous crime at tea time. The older you are when children come along, the more mature your approach in dealing with them. But in spite of this, you are still great fun to be with.

Sagittarius Mother
Throughout life you prize independence, but find it a little hard to adjust when the first child arrives. You encourage youngsters to stand on their own two feet earlier than most mothers might and usually steer them in such ways quite early. Clearly, you are not possessive, but a liberal. When your child wants something, you allow it to help him or her learn early self-sufficiency.

Sagittarius Father
Rather cautious when your first baby is brought home, you gradually throw yourself into the swing of things, and then never stop. Because you so enjoy the company of children, you are always ready to help out on school visits or holiday trips. You make an excellent father as you have a live-and-let-live attitude towards everyone, including your offspring.

Capricorn
As parents, you work well together, cool, calm and collected all the time – on the surface. However, this apparently hard exterior hides a

centre that is so soft even you would be hard pushed believing it. Your children are your pride and joy. All your hopes and ambitions are built in to the way you bring them up.

Practical and realistic, with both feet always on the ground, you provide a comfortable home for children. But what they badly need is for you to show a little more physical affection, to know you really love and care for them. Cuddles mean so much to a child so do not be stingy with them.

Capricorn Mother
The first working mum must have been a Capricorn. You can be so organised you make motherhood look easy. In a very short time you will lay down all the ground rules and have perfectly well-behaved children. Occasionally, you seem unable to relax. Children can have a hard time getting to know you closely.

Capricorn Father
You always have to be in control and are rather strict in matters of discipline. You can seem aloof to a child who looks up at you, perhaps a little unsure of how you are going to react when they speak to you. It is not intended: it is just how you come over to youngsters. Your overall attitude is rather conservative. This is unhelpful when they become teenagers.

Aquarians
All Aquarians are controversial. You do your own thing when you choose. But this does not stop when you become parents. One thing is sure: no child is ever going to be lonely or bored with you. Even a neighbour's youngster thrives in your house because you are so unpredictable.

As parents, you ensure you share everything with your children, right down to your ambitions for them and more. You really do not mind what they want to do, but are sage enough to point out the pitfalls. Then you let them make their own beds, but are there to pick up the pieces if it all goes wrong.

Aquarian Mother
Surprisingly, you can be rather strict when necessary, but once that is

over, your love of change and anything new takes on a fresh meaning for your children. You encourage them to experiment all the time. No one must say to you they do not like anything because they haven't tried it. They must attempt it first. If they don't like it, so be it.

Aquarian Father

It is second nature for you to be constantly on the go, juggling with this, that and the other, so when the first child arrives it takes time to fit them into your busy schedule. Then the fun really begins because they like your unconventional approach.

However, you must demonstrate your real feelings and not just a surface bonhomie. Children like to know they are loved. Show them!

Pisces

Parenthood is rather wearing on the true Pisces character. Of course, you will find it much harder than anything else you have ever undertaken because it is not in your nature to spend time looking after anyone on a permanent basis. You tend to be self-indulgent, doing what you want to do when it suits you.

After children come along, you have to knuckle down and try to make the best of things. Curiously, you make very good parents because eventually it all becomes so natural. You just do not like the hassle. You need to be organised and prepared to sacrifice, not exactly strong points with either of you.

Pisces Mother

Very much a child yourself, whatever your age. You soon learn when, where and how to do the shopping, plan ahead and remember to prepare junior for school.

You provide a loving home in which any child will be happy. It may not be neat and tidy, but has that lived-in feeling. You are likely to develop an almost psychic link with your youngsters, wherever they are.

Pisces Father

The role of being a father is rather scary at first, but once the mystery of caring and nurturing becomes second nature you rise to the occasion beautifully.

Later, discipline is likely to become non-existent. You may turn this over to your spouse. The general tendency is to want to keep the peace at all times and make sure the children do as you say, not necessarily as you do.